J. PATRICK KAPSCH

A LAYMAN'S THOUGHTS ON
HOLY SCRIPTURE

Copyright ©2025 by J. Patrick Kapsch
A Layman's Thoughts on Holy Scripture / J. Patrick Kapsch

ISBN Paperback: 978-1-943027-80-4
ISBN eBook: 978-1-943027-81-1

Published by Electric Moon Publishing

All rights reserved. No part of this publication may be reproduced, distributed, or transmitted in any form or by any means, including photocopying, recording, or other electronic or mechanical methods, without the prior written permission of the publisher, except in the case of brief quotations embodied in critical reviews and certain other noncommercial uses permitted by copyright law. For permission requests, write to the publisher, addressed at the address below:

Electric Moon Publishing
P.O. Box 96
Bonner Springs, KS 66012
www.emoonpublishing.com

Ordering information for print editions: Quantity sales. Special discounts are available on quantity purchases by corporations, associations, and others. For details, check out at *jpdakapsch@everestkc.net*

All Scripture quotations, unless otherwise indicated, are taken from the Holy Bible, New International Version®, NIV®. Copyright ©1973, 1978, 1984, 2011 by Biblica, Inc.™ Used by permission of Zondervan. All rights reserved worldwide. www.zondervan.com. The "NIV" and "New International Version" are trademarks registered in the United States Patent and Trademark Office by Biblica, Inc.™

Scripture quotations marked "KJV" are taken from the King James Version of the Holy Bible.

Electric Moon Publishing logos are tegistered trademarks of Electric Moon Publishing & Media, LLC and Hyperion Nebula Publishing Group, LLC.

Cover design: D.E. West - www.emoondesigns.com
Interior design: Stephanie Booth-Varnado - emoondesigns.com

Printed in the United States of America

www.emoonpublishing.com

DEDICATION

In memoriam I want to acknowledge the influence of my good friend, Ralph Gundelfinger.

He was a man small in stature but large in wisdom. Ralph was well read; he was well traveled and profoundly serious about his faith.

By the time I became serious about my writing, he was up in years and confined to his home. At his request I sent him examples which he would critique but offer encouragement, as well. As time went on, he began recommending I publish this body of my work.

Now, I still feel the need to express my thanks for his wise counsel. Ralph, the world is a better place for you having been part of it.

TABLE OF CONTENTS

Dedication iii
Table of Contents v
Foreward vii
Introduction IX

The Culprit 1
Why? 5
The Baptism of Jesus 9
Seeing is Believing 13
The Wedding Feast at Cana 17
A History Lesson 21
The Power of THE Word 25
Role Reversal 29
Jesus Heals a Paralytic 33
A Close Look at the Parable 37
A Story Within 41
Stepping Stones 45
The Our Father Prayer 49
Judge Not 53
Double Doubts 57
Don't We Need More? 61
The Greatest Parable 65
Parable of the Mustard Seed 69
Keep Searching 73
Don't Give Up. Don't Ever Give Up! 77
Sometimes I Wonder 81
The Doctrine of the Cross 85
The Transfiguration 89
Choices 93

Faith: How Much is Enough? 95
Winners and Loser 99
The Question 103
My Different Thoughts 107
The Ten Lepers 111
The Great Delay 115
Taking a Closer Look 119
My Man—Bartimeus 123
Are You Just a Fig Leaf? 127
The Marriage Feast 131
Judas the Iscariot–Why? 135
What Does it Mean to be Prepared? 139
Walking the Final Mile With Jesus 143
The Letter to the Romans 149
The Resurrection 153
Last But Not Least 157
No Time to Relax 161
Pentecost 165

Afterword 169

FOREWARD

In the book of Ephesians, Paul tells us that through *faith* we have been given "every spiritual blessing in Christ." Yet, we all live divorced from the reality. We spend much time focused on our worries and fears and not enough time on the abundance that is ours in *faith*.

Perhaps it is because we live in a culture that floods us with a message which focuses on what we lack, where we have failed and what we are missing.

The Kingdom of God is the opposite; *more is less and less is more. The first is last and the last is first. Eternal is forever; now is fleeting.* But how do we cling to this model despite the flood of counter messaging we experience every day? In other words, where do we seek *fulfillment and truth* in a world that feeds us false idols and empty promises?

I offer a simple solution: **scripture**. What we know about the things of this world is that they offer promises which are then not kept. *Scripture*, instead is "God-breathed." (2 Timothy 3:16) "a lamp to my feet and a light to my path." (Psalm 119:105) "*It gives endurance, encouragement and hope.*" (Romans 15:4) And "it is lasting." (Isaiah 40:8) It is an endless reminder of the *spiritual blessings* that Paul so repeatedly assured us we have in Christ.

My Grandpa Pat believed in the wisdom and guidance that Scripture offers. So much so that he spent an abundance of time reading, studying, and reflecting on its passages, both those well-known and those not so well-known. The pages that follow is a compilation of his thoughts and conclusions. As stated to me, in penning *his reflections*, he had three goals: That they be brief, interesting, and inspirational. As one who has read each one of them, I can state that they are, indeed, all three. Yet, to me, they are so much more; they tell of a heart captivated by God's Word, its complexity yet inherent simplicity all at once worthy of his time.

Dear reader, I sincerely hope his efforts will lead you to do likewise.

Kate Frerking, J.D.

INTRODUCTION

Some years back, while flipping through a book in the library, a line on one of the pages grabbed my attention: "Heaven and earth will pass away, but my words will never pass away." (Matthew 24:35)

Although I was raised in a Christian home and attended church regularly, I must admit, I never really listened intently as the Word was being proclaimed. Oh sure, I knew the readings were from the Bible, but that was about as close as I got to that book. Growing up, we were never schooled in Holy Scripture.

However, after that sentence got my attention, I thought about it and concluded that if Jesus' words will, indeed, endure forever they are worthy of my time to read and reflect on them.

I tried reading the Bible but found it difficult. I used several different approaches but never found one that really worked for me. The Books of the Old Testament were especially difficult to understand, and I struggled to find meaning in St. Paul's letters in the New Testament.

Over time, I found I got the greatest satisfaction from picking out a passage from one of the four Gospels which describes either a miracle performed by Jesus or a parable he used in his teaching and, after reading it, spending some time reflecting on it. Eventually, I began writing my thoughts down which led me to where I am today.

My hope is that you will find that these reflections will be easy to read and understand. I purposely kept them short, recognizing that, today, few people have a lot of time to devote to this form of prayer.

What I have written down are just *my thoughts*. There is no intent for my words to favor any one Christian denomination or to be doctoral in any manner.

Quite likely, after reading a reflection, you will have your own views on a subject matter and/or draw your own conclusions; regardless, it is my sincere hope you will be motivated to spend more time with Jesus' *words*.

1
The Culprit

Although, admittedly, not a student of the Old Testament, it occurred to me that I needed to go there before launching into a collection of reflections on the *Words and Actions* of Jesus during his earthly sojourn. Why was it necessary? To answer that question, I identified and dug into the Book of Genesis, specifically Chapters two and three. We will proceed on the assumption that the story, as shown in the Bible, is accurate.

Two key points to keep in mind as we continue:

1. The Devil has existed since the beginning of time.

2. God created man and woman with an intellect and free will.

Genesis 2

> *And the Lord formed man from the slime of the earth, and breathed into his face the breath of life and man became a living soul. (Genesis 2:7)*

And the Lord God had planted a paradise of pleasure wherein he placed the man whom he had formed.

And the Lord God brought forth of the ground all manner of trees fair to behold and pleasant to eat of. The tree of life also in the midst of paradise; and the tree of knowledge of good and evil.

And the Lord God took man and put him into the paradise of pleasure to dress it and to keep it.

And he commanded him saying: "OF every tree of paradise thou shall eat; but the tree of knowledge of good and evil thou shalt not eat. For in what day soever thou shalt eat of it thou shalt die the death." (Genesis 2:15–17)

Then the Lord God cast a deep sleep upon Adam and when he was fast asleep, he took out one of his ribs and filled up flesh.

And Adam said: "This now is bone of my bones and flesh of my flesh; she shall be called woman because she was taken out of man." (Genesis 2:22–23)

Genesis 3

Now the serpent was more subtle than any of the beasts of the earth which the Lord God had made. And he said to the woman: "Why hath God commanded you that you should not eat of every tree of paradise?"

And the woman answered him saying: "the trees that are in paradise we do eat; but of the fruit of the tree, which is in the midst of paradise, God hath com-

manded us that we should not eat, and we should not touch it lest perhaps we die."

And the serpent said to the woman: "No you shall not die the death. For God doth know that in what day soever you shall eat thereof, your eyes shall be opened, and you shall be as God, knowing good and evil."

And the woman saw that the tree was good to eat and fair to the eyes and delightful to behold; and she took of the fruit thereof and did eat and gave to her husband who did eat.

And the eyes of them both were opened, and they perceived themselves to be naked.

And when they heard the voice of the Lord God walking in the paradise of pleasure, they hid themselves from the face of the Lord God; for they were naked.

And he said to him: "And who hath told you that thou wast naked, **BUT THAT THOU HAST EATEN OF The TREE WHEREOF I COMMANDED THEE THAT THOU SHOULDST NOT EAT.**"

And Adam said: "The woman whom thou gavest me to be my companion, gave me of the tree, and I did eat."

And the Lord God said to the woman; "Why has thou done this?" and she answered: "The serpent deceived me, and I ate."

And the Lord God said to the serpent: "Because thou has done this thing, thou are **cursed among all cattle and beasts of the earth. UPON THY BREAST**

SHALT THOU CRAWL and earth shalt thou eat all the days of thy life."

And to Adam he said: "Because thou hast hearkened to the voice of your wife and hast eaten of the tree WHEREOF I COMMANDED THEE THAT THOU SHOULDST NOT EAT, CURSED IS THE EARTH IN THY WORK; WITH LABOUR AND TOIL SHALT THOU EAT THEREOF ALL THE DAYS OF THY LIFE." (Genesis 3:1–17)

And the Lord God sent him out of the paradise of pleasure, to till the earth from which he was taken.

ADAM and EVE in NOT HEEDING the COMMAND of the LORD GOD were guilty of sin: THE ORIGINAL SIN

Clearly, many centuries have come and gone since that first sin. And there is ample evidence in Scripture of the sinful words and actions of mankind throughout those years. Can we also agree that the serpent (Devil) is as active today in offering us temptations to "forbidden pleasure" as he/she was in the Garden? AND, the Lord God, despite our failings, still allows us to CHOOSE; and, in our failings, we are all sinners.

A Savior was needed then as well as now!

But note this also: The Lord God said to the serpent, **"I will put enmities between thee and the woman, and between THY SEED AND HER SEED; SHE SHALL CRUSH THY HEAD, AND THOU SHALT LIE IN WAIT FOR HER HEEL."**

Scripture scholars contend that it is her seed, **JESUS CHRIST**, by which the woman crushes the serpent's head. Therein, lies our hope for salvation.

2
Why?

Why does an infinitely loving God allow the terrible suffering we see everywhere in our world today? My answer to that question is: I DON'T KNOW! And, from the research I have done, NO ONE ELSE KNOWS EITHER!

Our initial challenge then, is to acknowledge and accept that suffering exists without doubting God's love.

And, can we agree, that God did not create suffering? Let's remember what we read in Genesis 1:31: And God saw all the things that he had made; and they were very good.

So, what happened? We return to Genesis 2:22: And the Lord cast a deep sleep upon Adam; and when he was fast asleep, he took one of his ribs and built the rib into a woman. Further, Genesis 3: 3-6: And the woman saw that the tree was good to eat and fair to the eyes and delightful to behold and *she took of it thereof and did eat of the forbidden fruit and gave to her husband who did eat.*

We have been taught from our youth that God created man and put him in charge of every living creature. In the Book of Deuteronomy, we find this: I have set before you life and death, blessings, and curses. Now **choose** life so that you and your children may live. (Deuteronomy 30:15–19)

Biblical scholars agree, suffering entered through man's exercise of his God given **free will**; therefore, we have Original Sin.

Now, having established that Adam and Eve chose "**curses**" and sin and "**death**," the apex of all pain and suffering, we return to our question: "Why does God **continue** to allow suffering in our world?" Since I still have not found an answer to that question, perhaps we should change our approach. Allow me to pose a different question: By the wording of the original question aren't we, in fact, hinting that we know better than God? Surely, we realize our understanding of God's ways, including suffering, is limited.

At this point in my study, I knew I needed to do further research to develop a better understanding of the background on this perplexing question. I started with the Old Testament, and with the Prophet Isaiah, Chapters 40–55. There, I read about the Jewish people whom God had just brought out of captivity. Indeed, Chapter 40 begins with the Prophet comforting the people with the promise of the coming of a Messiah to forgive their sins/sufferings. In that passage, we are introduced to the **Redemptive Jesus**. Further, in Chapter 42, God extols through the Prophet: "Behold thy **bold servant**; I will uphold him." **Our Servant Christ**, by virtue of his humanity is, also, the Servant of God. But the Jewish people were obstinate. Even so, God continued to promise an abundance of *spiritual gifts* (grace) to those who accepted his mercy. Then, we get a clue to the answer to our questions from Isaiah 55:8–9: "For my thoughts are not your thoughts, nor your ways my ways saith the Lord. For as the heavens are exalted above the earth, so are my ways exalted above your ways and my thoughts above your thoughts."

Circling back to our beginning question of WHY God allows suffering in our world, perhaps we should look inward; then, the question becomes is it God or is it us? Maybe there is an issue with our *understanding* of God's ways. Now, considering the preceding paragraph, shouldn't we accept that there is a *qualitative* difference between God's teaching on good and evil, right and wrong, etc. and our ability to comprehend that difference? In the end, perhaps the best **answer** is that we are just not capable of understanding God's ways. Finally, I suggest, that as a people of faith, we should never question God's ways and simply accept that our God is **all knowing** and **all loving**. And we should try to change our *attitude* toward our own suffering and the suffering we see all around us. Let us pray, then, that with the help of the Holy Spirit, we can come to understand that Jesus, by his death on the cross, has given a new meaning to the value of suffering by giving it a **preparatory quality**; and that we can accept our suffering as a **purifying step** to our meeting the **Suffering Jesus** face to face.

3

The Baptism of Jesus

Perhaps it was the winter doldrums, but, more likely, a spiritual hangover from Advent to Christmas to the Epiphany. Whatever the reason, the description, during Sunday readings, of the Baptism of Jesus never did capture my full attention; and it should have, because that Sunday marks the beginning of Ordinary Time on the Liturgical calendar. More importantly, it signals Jesus' passing from a private existence in Nazareth to a *very public* life in Galilee.

There is an old saying, "wherever you shall stumble, there you shall dig." Once spiritually awakened and digging, I was pleasantly surprised to find a worthwhile number of "nuggets" buried in Holy Scripture.

It is my hope that you will join me in this reflective exercise as I take a closer look at the event which was of sufficient importance to the early church that it is described in all four Gospels.

My research started with the Old Testament; there I found this: "the voice of one crying out in the desert; prepare ye the way of the Lord, make straight in the wilderness the path of our God." (Isaiah 40:3)

Then, I found in the New Testament, John the Baptist, himself a Prophet, was in the desert preaching a message of repentance for sins; and: "then there went out to him Jerusalem and all Judea and all the region about the Jordan and they were baptized by him in the Jordan River confessing their sins." (Matthew 3:5–6)

Jesus arrived and asked to be baptized; but John protested; "it is I who ought to be baptized by you." Jesus responded: "Let it be so now for it becomes us to fulfill all justice." Note that word– **fulfill**, we will look at it more closely later in our study; but here, I simply want to point out that in Greek or Aramaic, Matthew's native language, the word means to **accomplish or carry out**.

So, Jesus was baptized by John in the Jordan River; and immediately, on coming up out of the water, he saw the heavens opened and the Spirit, as a dove, descend and remain on him; and there came a voice from heaven: 'Thou art my beloved son; in THEE I am well pleased.'" (Mark 1:10–11)

I would also point out that this occasion marked the first time in the New Testament that the voice of the Father was heard. The next, and only other time more than one person heard His voice was the event of The Transfiguration of Jesus. At that time, there came a voice out of the cloud saying, "THIS is my beloved Son LISTEN TO HIM." (Matthew 17:35) I would also note that The Transfiguration took place much later in Jesus' ministry; and in that instance the Father said, "**LISTEN** to Him."

In addition, I found a more detailed description of Jesus' arrival from Nazareth in John's Gospel: John saw Jesus coming toward him and shouted: "behold the **Lamb of God** who takes away the sins of the world." (John 1:29–31) Therewith, John echoed Isaiah in proclaiming the coming of a Savior; **however**, there is another point to be made regarding John's version as opposed to the Synoptic Gospels; he refers to Jesus as the **Lamb**. It might be easy to gloss right over that difference since we have heard this Gospel many times; however, the reference to **Lamb** was a significant one, and most likely, would not have been lost on a mostly Jewish following; to them, reference to a lamb would, very likely, bring to mind the Jewish rite of sacrificing a lamb in the Holy Temple for atonement of their sins. However, John the Baptist was foreshadowing that Jesus, as the **Lamb of God**, would be sacrificed for the sins of all mankind.

I highlighted certain words as we went along to discern a deeper meaning so now let's return to the dialogue between John the Baptist and Jesus leading up to Jesus' baptism and, specifically on the word **FULFILL**.

I do not think that Jesus just happened to arrive at the Jordan River that day. This event, I believe, was part of the Father's "master plan" to set in motion His goal of *redemption* for all people. Jesus simply carried out the will of his Father. Recall the Father's words: "You are my beloved Son in whom I am well pleased." Jesus' baptism, therefore, was a *fulfillment*: "Let it be so now for it becomes us to fulfill all justice."

I also believe that Jesus chose to be baptized in the muddy waters of the Jordan, thereby beginning his Gospel of *mercy and forgiveness* by sharing in the water of sinners. Beautiful symbolism!

Finally, along with this *happening* of the Baptism of Jesus, we were also introduced to the great mystery of the Trinity: God the Father, Jesus the beloved Son and the Holy Spirit, in the form of a dove.

Thereafter, Jesus chose to go into the desert and undergo the Devil's temptations for 40 days. Upon returning to Galilee and learning of the arrest of John the Baptist, he proclaimed: "The time is **fulfilled**! The Kingdom of God is at hand. Repent and believe in the Gospel." (Mark 1:15)

And it all started with the Baptism of Jesus!

4

Seeing is Believing

Jesus worked 37 miracles during his time on earth; and most involved healing the sick, giving sight to the blind and driving out demons. This reflection, based on "catching fish" won't elicit much excitement; still, it involves a miracle and is one, I found, to be worthy of study. It is described only in Luke's Gospel.

To this point, Jesus had been baptized, spent forty days in the desert being tempted by the devil and taught extensively in their synagogue. At the end of Chapter four, we find Jesus trying to get some rest, but the crowds kept coming to him; that gets us to Chapter five and our passage for study:

> *Now it came to pass, while the crowds were pressing upon him to hear the word of God, that he was standing by Lake Genesareth. And he saw two boats moored by the lake, but the fishermen had left them and were washing their nets. And getting into one of the boats, the one that was Simon's, he asked him to*

> *put out a little from the land. And sitting down, he began to teach the crowds from the boat. But when he had ceased speaking, he said to Simon, "Put out into the deep and lower your nets for a catch." And Simon answered and said to him, "Master, the whole night through we have toiled and have taken nothing; but at thy word I will lower the net." And when they had done so, they enclosed a great number of fishes, but their net was breaking. And they beckoned to their comrades in the other boat to come and help them. And they came and filled both boats, so they began to sink. But when Simon Peter saw this, he fell down at Jesus' knees, saying, "Depart from me, for I am a sinful man, O Lord." For he and all who were with him were **amazed** at the catch of fish they had made; and so were also James and John, the sons of Zebedee, who were partners with Simon. And Jesus said to Simon, "Do not be afraid; henceforth thou shall catch men." And when they had brought their boats to land, they left all and followed him. (Luke 5:1–11)*

First note Simon's response to Jesus' request that they put out into the deep for a catch, "Master, the whole night through we have toiled and have taken nothing."

Simon questioned that Jesus' request would be fruitful; he **Doubted**. He did not **Believe**. The text suggests that Simon thought it was a waste of time; he had no idea of Jesus' **Divine power**. Then, he saw and *believed*.

Simon, respectfully, did as Jesus requested. He proceeded to do God's will. Afterward, Simon was *ashamed*! "Depart from me for I am a sinful man, O Lord." He fell at "Jesus' knees." Jesus said,

"Do not be afraid." He knew what Simon was going through and he had **compassion** for him.

This story reminds me of an old saying: There but for the grace of God go I. I have been in Simon's shoes. I tried and tried to accomplish a goal without success. I prayed and prayed. Perhaps you have had a similar experience. We pray and pray, but still no luck. Jesus reminds us in this passage to not give up and **understand** he has the **power** to solve our problem. As with Simon, he urges us to keep trying. We **must have faith** in his Divine power and **trust** in his willingness to help us. Never forget we are told to "knock and keep knocking."

This is a powerful little story which can be summed up in just a few key words:

**TRUST, FAITH, CONTRITION,
COMPASSION and DISCIPLESHIP**

5

The Wedding Feast at Cana

Recently, I heard proclaimed the passage from John's Gospel, which described Jesus turning *water into wine*. (John 2:1–11) Although it is one which I had heard many times, I decided to spend more time thinking about it to discern a message or messages therein.

Soon after I began my study, I realized that this miracle, or *sign* as it is designated in John's Gospel, is described ONLY in John's Gospel; none of the three Synoptic Gospel authors included it in their Gospels. I wondered about that; I believe I may have found the answer; I will offer it later.

Once I decide to look closely at a particular passage, I usually find it helpful to look at the scene preceding the event being studied to understand the background; all <u>four</u> Gospels report the arrival of Jesus into Galilee from Nazareth. What followed was **The Baptism of Jesus**, which was a significant event and, itself, worthy of a reflection. Interestingly, John did not describe that in his Gospel while ALL three of the Synoptic Gospel authors did include it. There had been speculation dating to the early church, that there were strained relations between the followers of John the Baptist and the apostles, including John which may or may not have been a factor. Be that as it may, let's move on to our subject passage, The Wedding Feast at Cana:

> *And on the third day a marriage took place at Cana of Galilee, and the* **mother** *of Jesus was there. Now Jesus too was invited to the marriage AND, also, his disciples. And the wine having run short, the mother of Jesus said to him: "They have no wine." And Jesus said to her: "What wouldst thou have me do, woman? My hour has not yet come"? His mother said to the attendants: "Do whatever he tells you to do."*

> *Now six stone water-jars were placed there after the Jewish manner of purification, each holding two or three measures. Jesus said to them, "fill the jars with water" and they filled them to the brim. And Jesus said to them, "Draw out now and take to the chief steward." And they took it to him. Now when the chief steward had tasted the water after it had become wine, not knowing whence it was (though the attendants who had drawn the water knew), the chief steward called the bridegroom and said to him: "Every man at first sets forth the good wine, and when they have drunk freely, then that which is poorer. But thou hast kept the good wine until now."*

> *This first of his signs Jesus worked at Cana of Galilee and he* **manifested his Glory** *and his disciples believed in him.*

Now to the question: Why did Matthew, Mark and Luke NOT include this miracle in their Gospels? My answer—WOMAN! I realize that may seem a bit strong, so I'll try to explain and offer supporting data.

To begin, it is important to note that in the prevailing Jewish culture, women were not held in high regard; in fact, women were considered to be inferior with no social stature. Their role was to provide offspring for their husbands. Thus, the Synoptic Gospel authors might well have felt Mary played too great of a role in the event and, that her instruction was *outside the norm*; therefore, not appropriate for the mostly Jewish communities for whom they were writing.

Then, that raised another question: Why did John describe the event and in such detail? In my view the answer to that question hits at the primary lesson of the passage. First, note: "and the mother of Jesus **was there**." That suggests to me that John, perhaps, knew she had a role of some kind at the ceremony and he, therefore, wanted to portray her in that greater stature. In addition, I conclude that John, with his detailed description, took this step early on in his Gospel to establish that Jesus held women in higher esteem than they were under Jewish law and custom. Further review showed that John followed this up in Chapter 4:7–26, with Jesus' conversation with the Samaritan woman at the well and at Chapter 8:1–11, the woman alleged to have been caught in the act of adultery.

One other aspect I noted was the way that John used the word ***woman*** in this passage, and, also, later in his Gospel. Recall, Jesus said to HIS mother, "what would you have me do **woman**?" That may seem a little disrespectful, but I do not think so; used in that context, I believe the **word** had a universal meaning. He was not addressing her as **HIS** mother but in a universal sense, as in the mother of **ALL**.

Finally, let us move to the foot of the cross where we read:

> *When Jesus, therefore, saw his mother and the disciple he loved standing by he said to his mother: "**woman** behold your son." (John 19:25–29)*

Indeed, he was thereby declaring her the universal mother of **all sons**!

This event offers us a wonderful lesson: Mary is our **universal** mother. We would do well to always remember her important words: DO WHATEVER HE TELLS YOU.

To summarize, Mary's role at the Wedding was the reason the Synoptic Gospel writers chose not to include this GREAT FIRST PUBLIC SIGN by Jesus. Also, the way it played out gave John precisely the material he wanted to portray Jesus in a different light toward women as opposed to the prevailing culture. Thereafter, in the Gospel of John, we find other women who played a role in Jesus' ministry, for example, Mary and Martha.

Finally, I like this story because it gives us a **first** and a last: at the Wedding Feast at Cana Jesus performed his first public miracle; and Mary's words, "do whatever he tells you." Those were her **last spoken words** in the Bible.

6

A History Lesson

Following Jesus' baptism by John the Baptist, we find this in Mark's Gospel: "And immediately the Spirit drove him forth into the desert. And he was in the desert forty days and forty nights being tempted the while by **SATAN**." (Mark 1:14–15)

After calling his disciples, he proceeded to Cana in Galilee where he worked his first miracle at a wedding; however, you would not know that from Mark's Gospel since he chose not to include that event; rather, he has Jesus in Capharnaum. The title for this reflection introduces us to that miracle in Mark's Gospel:

> Now in their Synagogue there was a man with an **unclean spirit**; and he cried out saying, "what have we to do with thee, Jesus of Nazareth, hast thou come to destroy us? I know who thou art, the Holy One of God." And Jesus rebuked him saying, "hold thy peace and go out of the man." And the **unclean spirit**, convulsing him and crying out in a loud voice went out of him. (Mark 1:21–28)

Interestingly, Luke, in his Gospel, describing the same event, wrote, "there was a man possessed by an **unclean DEVIL**." (Luke 4:33–36)

Mark has this event as Jesus' second miracle and one of four in which Jesus, himself, "heals someone with an **unclean spirit/ demon**."

Those terms, "Satan," "unclean devil," "evil spirit" and "demons" caught my attention, raised questions, and sent me searching for answers. I learned they are used somewhat interchangeably in Scripture; but where did they originate? Who are they? What are they?

Let's start with Satan whom we met in the first paragraph of this reflection. He was created by God who spoke of such through the Prophet Isaiah: "I form the light and create darkness. I made peace and created **evil**." (Isaiah 45:7) Indeed, Satan was once an angel of God, known as Lucifer; but he rebelled against God.

And then this from Isaiah: "How art thou fallen from heaven, O Lucifer, who didst rise in the morning? How art thou fallen to earth that thou didst wound the nations"? (Isaiah 14:12) Lucifer is best known from the Book of Revelation where he appeared as a dragon who sought to devour the newborn child. There, then, was a battle in heaven; Michael, the archangel, and his angels battled with the dragon and the dragon fought back with his angels; and they did not prevail! Neither was their place anymore in heaven. That great dragon was cast down, the **ancient serpent**, he who is called the **devil** and **Satan** who leads astray the whole world; and he was cast down to earth and with him his angels were cast down. (Revelation 12:7–9)

Thus, we can conclude that "demons" and "unclean spirits" are angels of Satan.

Next, my study led me to this passage of considerable interest: "Then having summoned his twelve disciples, he gave them power over **unclean spirits** to cast them out and to cure every kind of disease and infirmity." (Matthew 10:1) In Luke we have similar but slightly different wording, "he gave them power and authority over the **devils** and to cure diseases." (Luke 9:1)

HOWEVER, that power was NOT without limits. In other words, his disciples did not receive the **power of Jesus**, especially in situations involving the **Devil**. Example: "Lord have pity on my son, for he is a lunatic and suffers severely, for often he falls into the fire and often into the water. I brought him to thy disciples, but *they could not cure him*." Jesus said, "bring him to me." And Jesus rebuked him, and the **DEVIL** went out of him. (Matthew 17:14–17)

And again: "Master, I have brought to thee my son who has a **dumb spirit** and whenever it seizes him it throws him down and he foams and grinds his teeth; and he is wasting away. And I told thy disciples to cast it out, *but they could not*." (Mark 9:16–17)

So, what are we to make of all this? An angel created by God rebelled, lost the fight with an archangel, was thrust down to earth along with his angels where they work to draw people away from God; look at Adam and Eve, tricked by the serpent/devil. We previously mentioned the devil's efforts to trick Jesus himself. So yes, the devil has shown himself to be present throughout history, as documented in scripture. From events noted herein, it is clear the devil **retains his power to possess**.

It is not difficult to find evidence of the Devil in our world today; he seems to have had considerable success dumbing down morality to near non-existence in our culture. Unfortunately, he is currently having success in convincing Christians, especially, our younger generation, that attending church is not only unnecessary, but not worth their time. Our society, today, affords him unlimited opportunity to get people to lower their guard with promises of money, power, and pleasures of all kinds. We know from these passages in Scripture, *he was there*, and we know, as well, he *IS HERE TODAY*.

Jesus said: "This kind can be cast out in no way except by prayer and fasting." (Mark 9:29)

TO BE FOREWARNED IS TO BE FOREARMED!

7

The Power of *THE* Word

First, I want to make clear that there is NOT a typing error in the title. Hopefully, that will be evident as we work our way through this reflection.

The passage for this study is Chapter 4:43–54 from the Gospel of John; it reads as follows:

> *Now after two days he departed from that place and went into Galilee, for Jesus himself bore witness that a prophet receives no honor in his own country. When, therefore, he had come into Galilee, the Galileans received him, having seen all that he had done in Jerusalem during the feast, for they had also gone to the feast.*
>
> *He came again therefore to Cana of Galilee, where he had made water into wine. And there was a certain royal official whose son was lying sick at Capharnaum. When he heard that Jesus had come from Judea into Galilee, he went to him and besought him to*

> *come down and heal his son, for he was at the point of death.*
>
> *Jesus therefore said to him, "Unless you see signs and wonders, you do not believe." The royal official said to him, "Sir, come down before my child dies." Jesus said to him, "Go thy way, thy son **lives**."*
>
> *The man **believed** the **WORD** that Jesus spoke to him and departed. But even as he was now going down, his servants met him and brought word saying that his son lived. He asked of them therefore the hour in which he got better. And they told him, "Yesterday, at the seventh hour, the fever left him." The father knew then that it was **at that very hour** in which Jesus had said to him, "Thy son **lives**." And he himself believed and his whole household.*

Once again, we find that the Synoptic Gospel authors did not include this miracle in their Gospels; it is described only in John's Gospel which is not that surprising since his Gospel, as opposed to the other Gospels, tended more toward dialogue than action. So, this story fits well with one of the goals of his Gospel: that there be an emphasis on "faith/belief" and "hope."

The first few chapters of John's Gospel read like a geography lesson; Jesus goes from Nazareth to Galilee to Jerusalem then to Cana in Galilee, to Judea to Bethany to Samaria and back to Cana. Now, here in Chapter 4, we have a royal official coming up from Capharnaum to catch up with Jesus. I learned that it is 16 miles!

The royal official had a son who was extremely sick–at the point of death. He made that journey because he was desperate to save his son AND he **thought** Jesus could **heal** him; AND Jesus did.

However, let's take a closer look at the dialogue between them: The official *beseeched Jesus to COME DOWN*; to make that 16 mile trip! But Jesus rebuked him, "Unless you see signs and wonders you do not believe." The royal official persisted, "Sir, *come down before my child dies."* Jesus said to him, "Go thy way, thy son lives." With HIS prayer, the man thought he could dictate to Jesus **how** (*come down*) and **when** (*now*) to respond to his request/prayer. Jesus answered his prayer: "GO, thy son lives." (Jesus: *I didn't NEED to be THERE*; but it was necessary to measure the depth of your **faith** in my Divine power.)

Upon learning about the miracle of the **healing** of his son, "he himself **believed** and his whole household."

So, we followed the *desperate hope* of the royal official, who initially saw Jesus as just a healer, become a *true believer*—seeing Jesus as the Christ, God, and Savior! And, as indicated, John viewed the event as completely consistent with the overriding purpose for writing his Gospel; NOTE: *these/signs have been written so that you may believe that Christ is the Son of God and that believing you have **life** in His name.* (John 21:25)

And for us, questions remain: Do we only pray when we really need something? When we do pray, what is the level of our faith? As we turn to Jesus with our prayer is it *shallow* (hoping) or *believing* (He is the Christ, the Son of God)? If you answered "believing," is your faith such that it leads others to Jesus?

FAITH SHARED IS FAITH REWARDED!

8

Role Reversal

What we have here is a Jesus miracle where he healed a man suffering from the dreaded disease of *leprosy*. It should be noted that in that culture, a person suffering from the disease was subject to strict social guidelines; one suspected of having the condition MUST present to a Priest for inspection and, after a period of monitoring, and if not improved, was declared unclean. Thereafter, the person was ostracized from society and forced to live outside the community in a camp and STRICTLY forbidden from any non-leper contact.

I believe it is also important to point out that this miracle occurred near the beginning of Jesus' earthly ministry.

The event is described in all three Synoptic Gospels, but with some interesting differences. Matthew, in his Gospel, has the setting as Jesus having just descended from the mountain after delivering his *Sermon on the Mount*; Mark and Luke do not connect the verse with the *Sermon*. In the end, I feel it best to study the passage as it is described in Mark's Gospel:

*And a leper came to him, entreating him and kneeling down he said," if thou wilt, thou **canst make me clean."** And Jesus having compassion on him stretched forth his hand and **touched him**, and said to him, "I will; be thou made **clean."** And when he had spoken, immediately the leprosy left him, and he was made clean. Then he strictly CHARGED him and immediately **drove him away**. And he said to him. "See thou tell no one; but go show thyself to the priest and offer thy purification the things Moses commanded for a witness to them." But he went out and began to publish and to spread abroad the fact, so that Jesus **could no longer openly enter a town but remained outside in desert places**. (Mark 1:40–49)*

Comments:

As noted earlier, Jesus was just getting started on his mission to preach to All PEOPLES that the *Kingdom of God was at hand*. He had MUCH MORE to do and say before being glorified by his death and resurrection. Jesus' **compassion** was of utmost importance. He not only WILLED the healing but **touched** the leper.

Let's look carefully at Jesus' unusually strongly worded instruction to the healed man: HE STRICTLY CHARGED HIM AND IMMEDIATELY DROVE HIM AWAY and said to him, "**SEE THOU TELL NO ONE**." Jesus knew what would happen if word got out; large crowds, at some point, would seize him and declare him their long-awaited king.

But let us also look closely at the leper: He entreated him (bowed lowly) and knelt before him. Moreover, he knew Jesus had the power to heal him; he said, "**if thou WILT**." THAT WAS HIS PRAYER! Clearly, he was a man of FAITH. This former leper then became a **disciple** by spreading the *WORD*. Finally, consider the reversal that took place within this story: The realities of the leper and Jesus are switched; the leper who ought not enter his community without being freed from his ailment RETURNS to his village and his previous way of life. On the other hand, Jesus is suddenly unable to enter a village and is kept from his intended role of preaching to many potential believers.

Lessons:

Jesus is ALWAYS close by, ready to cleanse us from the illness of sin. This story offers us a template for prayer: *KNEEL, OFFER HOMAGE* and *HUMBLY ASK* that it might be his will that our prayer "wilt" be granted.

Now with his CRUCIFIXION and RESURRECTION we, too, should be active disciples and "**spread the word**" by the way we live our lives.

9
Jesus Heals a Paralytic

This is a *nice* story on several levels; but for me, it borders on not believable. As we work our way through this passage, I am confident you, too, will have questions, if not doubts. Interestingly, it is described in all three Synoptic Gospels; John does not include it in his Gospel as I believe he was more inclined toward Jesus' *dialogue* than his physical *action*.

I will state, upfront, that I do accept that Sacred Scripture is the *inspired word of God*, however, there is no information here that these three authors were witnesses to this event. Who or what was their source? Given the circumstances, as described, I would think the source would have been verbal. Then, one must factor in that these stories were written several generations after the miracle took place, increasing the probability of misunderstanding and/or misinterpretation. Therefore, I do not accept a literal reading of the Bible.

This event took place quite early in Jesus' earthly ministry. We will utilize Mark's version which is found at Chapter 2:1–12; Mark has been *tabbed the action author* which lends itself to this story. I do feel it is necessary to include the entire passage in order not to leave out key details:

> *And after some days, he again entered Capharnaum, and it was reported that he was at home. And many gathered together so that there was no longer room, not even around the door. And he spoke the word to them. And they came bringing to him a paralytic carried by four. And since they could not bring him to Jesus because of the crowd, they stripped off the roof where he was, and, having made an opening, they let down the pallet on which the paralytic was lying. And Jesus seeing their faith said to the paralytic, "Son, thy sins are forgiven thee."*
>
> *Now some of the Scribes were sitting there and reasoning in their hearts: "Why does can forgive sins but only God?" And, at once, Jesus knowing in his spirit that they so reasoned within themselves, said to them, "Why are you arguing these things in your hearts? Which is easier to say to the paralytic thy sins are forgiven thee or to say: Arise, and take up thy pallet and walk'? But that you might know that the Son of Man has power on earth to forgive sins–he said to the paralytic: "I say to thee arise, take up thy pallet, and go to thy house." And immediately he arose and, taking up his pallet, went forth in the sight of all, so that they were all amazed, and glorified God, saying, "Never did we see the like."*

Just a quick reminder, in that culture, an illness or disease was thought to have resulted from the sins of either the afflicted person or his parents.

I stated at the outset that this is a *nice* STORY on *several* levels. So, let's look at those levels:

Faith

Whose faith—the four friends/carriers who went to great lengths to get their friend to Jesus with **bold** faith that he would heal him OR the faith of the paralytic? Jesus answered that question; he had noted **their faith** by addressing the paralytic: "**Son, thy sins are forgiven thee**."

Condemnation

The Scribes sitting there and reasoning in their hearts: Why does this man speak thus? He **blasphemes**. Who can forgive sins but only God?

Divinity

Jesus **knowing in his spirit** that they so reasoned, said to them, "Why are you arguing those things **in your hearts**? Which is easier to say, to the paralytic, thy sins are forgiven thee? Or to say: Arise, and take up thy pallet and walk?"

Power

But that you may know that the Son of Man has **power on earth to forgive sins**, he said to the paralytic: "I say to thee **arise, take up thy pallet and go** to thy house."

Healing

"Son, thy sins are forgiven thee. Arise, take up thy pallet and go."

And immediately he **arose and taking up his pallet went forth. Jesus healed the soul before he healed the body**!

Clearly, this passage is, primarily, about Faith; but did the friends actually go through the roof? Common sense tells me they did not. I believe Mark used hyperbole for action. Of course. Also, he wanted to emphasize **faith as it relates to miraculous healing**.

Matthew didn't include the "roof" in his Gospel and Luke, as usual, just copied Mark.

Regardless, let us pray that God will grant us **FAITH** such that we never doubt the power of Jesus to heal/help and that we stand ready, in prayer and action, to be there for our friends and neighbors in his or her hour of need.

10

A Close Look at the Parable

We know Jesus often used parables as a tool in his teaching. In fact, he did so on 39 to 50 occasions depending on which source you accept. They can be found in all three Synoptic Gospels; John did not include parables.

I indicated in my introduction that we would study some of those occasions to discern what message Jesus was trying to convey.

We find our first such occasion in Mark's Gospel; there we encounter old versus new. However, before we dig into that event, I feel we should examine what the parable, as utilized by Jesus, was all about. I found these explanations for consideration:

> *"At its simplest the parable is a metaphor or simile drawn from nature or common life arresting the hearer by its vividness or strangeness and leaving the mind insufficient about its precise application to tease it into active thought."* C.H. Dodd

If that seems as heavy to you as it does to me, let's try this:

> *"Jesus explained that for those who have ears to hear, the parable provides a deeper understanding of Jesus' teaching. But for those who do not have ears to hear, the parable is actually an instrument of concealment. The parable was not given simply to make everything clear to people; it was also given to obscure meaning to those who are outside who are not given understanding. That sounds somewhat harsh; Jesus came not only to instruct and to help people understand the kingdom of God. He came also as a judgement on those who do not want to hear the truth." R.C. Sproul*

This latter view will make more sense once you see that at the time Jesus began using the parable in his teaching the Scribes and Pharisees, Jewish religious leaders, were already challenging him whenever possible. That will become apparent as we look at the following event.

We will begin our study of the parable in Mark's Gospel, 2:13–22. Inasmuch as Jesus was just beginning in his public ministry, the context needed comes from Jesus calling Levi, a tax collector, to be an apostle. We would come to know him as Matthew. After the calling and acceptance, Jesus dined at Matthew's house which prompted the Scribes and Pharisees to ask Jesus' disciples, "Why does your master eat and drink with sinners and publicans"?

Next challenge:

> *The disciples of John and the Pharisees were fasting. And they came and said to him, "Why do the disciples of John and the Pharisees fast, whereas thy disciples do not fast"? And Jesus said to them, "Can the wedding guests fast if the bridegroom is with them? If*

> they have the bridegroom with them, they cannot fast. But the days will come when the bridegroom shall be taken away from them and then they will fast on that day." (Mark 2:19)

Therewith, Jesus compares his coming to that of a bridegroom to his wedding; during that time of joy no one thinks of fasting.

> Then Jesus said, "**No one sews a patch of raw cloth on an old garment; else the new patch tears away from the old and a worse rent is made.** And no one pours new wine into old wine skins; else the wine will burst the skins and the wine will be spilt and the skins will be ruined. But new wine must be put into fresh skins." (Mark 2:22)

Jesus, addressing his followers, but with the Jewish leaders listening, as well, was saying his message represents a **New Covenant** which they should not try to use to attach to or repair the *Old Covenant*.

As the Jewish religious leaders zero in on every word and action by Jesus, he responds on this occasion by using metaphors, such as a bridegroom, as well as garments and wineskins, to try to explain to the crowds following him that he offers a different way of thinking; his **WORD** represents an ORDER of love and forgiveness versus the *OLD COVENANT* representing the Mosaic Law. Jesus did not come to repair, improve, or update Judaism. Judaism was worn out. Jesus brought something entirely new: New garment, New wineskin. New way.

The institutes of Christ and those of the Pharisees could never be brought to accord. As with the garment and the wineskins, doing so would be unwise.

11

A Story Within

As I was reading John's Gospel, it occurred to me that he spent a lot of time on words to tell the stories surrounding Jesus' miracles, or signs, as John called them.

For this reflection, we will look at the miracle/sign where Jesus healed a man who had suffered from his infirmity for 38 years and who was lying by a pool in Jerusalem, called in Hebrew, Bethsaida; it was known for its "healing" water. (John 5:1–18)

This event took place quite early in Jesus' earthly ministry and, interestingly, is described only in John's Gospel. To set the scene:

- Chapter One—Jesus arrives in Galilee and is baptized by John the Baptist.

- Chapter Two—Jesus changes water to wine at a Wedding in Cana.

- Chapter Three—Nicodemus, a Pharisee, and a Jewish ruler visits Jesus.

- Chapter Four—The Samaritan woman meets Jesus at the well.

As usual, John was generous with details so I will paraphrase in the interest of brevity:

> Jesus went up to Jerusalem for a Jewish Feast—Passover. He passed by the Bethsaida where the sick, blind, lame and those with shriveled limbs were awaiting an angel to arrive to *stir up the water for healing*; thereafter, the first person into the pool would be cured.
>
> Jesus was passing, saw a man and *knowing he had been in this state for a long time*, he said to him, "Dost thou want to get well?" The man explained that no one would take him into the pool. Jesus said to him, "Rise, take up thy pallet and walk." And, at once the man was cured. And he took up his pallet and walked.
>
> Jesus quietly walked away.

That day was the Sabbath!

> The man did not know Jesus. He thought he could only be healed by getting in the pool. Even after Jesus healed him, he still told the Jewish religious leaders he did not know the man who healed him.
>
> Jesus, later, **found** the man in the temple and said to him, "Behold, thou art cured! **Sin no more** lest something worse befall thee."

The man informed the Jewish religious leaders it was Jesus who told him to "take up his pallet and walk." **They then began persecuting him as a violator of the Sabbath.**

Jesus answered the Jews: "**MY FATHER** works even until now, and **I Work**."

The Jews were the more anxious **to put him to death** because he not only, broke the Sabbath, but **he also called God his own Father**.

This is, indeed, a perplexing story. For me, the real question is: **WHY DID JESUS DO WHAT HE DID WHEN HE DID IT?**

Thoughts to consider:

- The man did not ask to be healed; he did not even know Jesus. Jesus initially healed the man physically, NOT spiritually.

- Jesus knew that under Mosaic law that he was precluded from healing on the Sabbath. He also knew it was NOT lawful for one to carry his mat.

My conclusions:

- This took place early in his public ministry and Jesus wished to "announce" publicly that HE WAS THE SON OF MAN!

- He instigated this "dust-up" with the Jewish religious leaders. He knew they would challenge him for breaking the Sabbath. He knew that forgiving the man's sins would anger the Pharisees. He called God his own father which the Jews called blaspheming. He knew that everything he said or did was to carry out the will of his Father.

12

Stepping Stones

In this reflection, my intent was to study and write down my thoughts on Jesus' teaching at the Sermon on the Mount considered by many to be the cornerstone of Christian ethics and teachings. As soon as I began my research, I realized that the Sermon on the Mount covers three Chapters in Matthew's Gospel. With a quick overview it became apparent there was no way to write about that entire event and stay within my self-imposed boundary for brevity. So, we will proceed to study and write about just Chapter 5—The Beatitudes.

The Webster's Dictionary defines **Beatitude** as the following: supreme blessedness; exalted happiness. This is consistent with Jesus' approach in teaching his disciples, and us, how to be holy. Being **holy** = being **happy**. Specifically, the Beatitudes outline qualities and attitudes valued in the Kingdom of Heaven.

The Beatitudes:

Blessed are the poor in spirit for theirs is the kingdom of heaven.

In spiritual terms it means always putting God first. It is a prerequisite for holiness. One could also consider poor in spirit as the opposite of pride—giving versus receiving. This is not to be confused with economic poverty. Understanding this Beatitude is critical to understanding the other seven.

Blessed are the meek for they shall inherit the earth.

We should not confuse meek with weakness. It does mean one gets his strength from God and is obedient to God. The Lord God's love for them is supported by the Prophet Isaiah: "The spirit of the Lord is upon me because the Lord hath anointed me. He hath sent me to preach to the meek." (Isaiah 61)

Blessed are they who mourn for they shall be comforted.

Jesus is speaking about their sinfulness and the need to "mourn" or repent. This Beatitude points to the state of being separated from God due to sin and yearning for and seeking Christ. In the spiritual sense mourning/sorrow is the first step to repentance. They shall be comforted is the natural result of repentance which leads to holiness.

Blessed are they who hunger and thirst for justice for they shall have their fill.

One might read this as hunger and thirst for righteousness. The first step requires one to admit one's NEED and have the DESIRE to be close to God. What are YOU hungry for? Remember this from Scripture: He has filled the hungry with good things and the rich he has sent away empty. (Luke 1:53)

Blessed are the merciful for they shall obtain mercy.

Mercy is what God is!! To be truly merciful is to become "God-like". Mercy is an active virtue that Christians can show each other because we have received Mercy. "Therefore, be merciful, just as your Father is merciful." (Luke 6:36)

Blessed are the pure of heart for they shall see God.

This is often referred to as a clean heart. To be able to resist the many temptations all around us does NOT make a **pure** heart although that is a good start. To have a **pure** heart, we must overcome our inner sins, i.e., pride, envy, selfishness, greed, hatred, etc. To see those inner sins, we need the light of Christ. With his help we CAN have a clear conscience, and a clear conscience equals a **pure** heart.

*Blessed are the **peacemakers** for they shall be called sons of God.*

The first step to being a **peacemaker** is to practice humility. Likewise, too much pride is an impediment to reaching those with whom you wish to assist. One must be at peace to make peace. A prerequisite to peace is to deny oneself and pray, asking the Prince of Peace to assist.

Blessed are those persecuted for righteousness's sake for theirs is God's place.

> If one actively lives out their Christian values, he/she will likely encounter resentment of one kind or another. Perhaps being shunned or ridiculed or faced with open criticism. The Prophets of old, the Apostles, and Jesus himself underwent persecution. Remember that Jesus said, "no servant is greater than his master. If they have persecuted me, they will persecute you also." (John 15:20)

Most scholars agree that the Beatitudes give us a picture of a true disciple of God. Accordingly, we Christians are challenged to use them as a "road map" for our lives, **stepping stones** to holiness, with the hope that in doing so we too might be rewarded.

13

The Our Father Prayer

How many times have you recited this prayer? Perhaps it is your favorite prayer. It is considered by many to be the greatest of all the prayers. Why? Because the words come from Jesus, himself.

Our reflection today is from Matthew's Gospel, Chapters 5 & 6. At that time, Jesus had just delivered his Sermon on the Mount and went off to pray alone. Upon returning to his apostles, one of them said, "Lord, teach us to pray." Jesus began his instruction by telling them **how not to pray**: "Don't multiply words as the Gentiles do thinking that God would be more likely to listen to a longer prayer." Then he said: "when you pray, you shall say, Our Father, hallowed be thy name. Thy Kingdom come Thy will be done. Give us this day our daily bread and forgive us our sins for we also forgive everyone who is indebted to us. And lead us not into temptation."

Scripture scholars suggest we should view the prayer as being made up of *Seven Petitions*; the first three being more theological in that they draw us toward God. The last four express our expectations of God.

In this study, we will attempt to discern the *meaning* of each of the seven petitions. To begin, this is **how** Jesus began his instruction: "when you pray, you *shall* say **OUR FATHER!**" Note, he did not say "my father" or "your father" or even, "just father" *but* **OUR FATHER**. Jesus wants us to view God as our *spiritual* father and to realize we are His children. We are **family, God's family**! Note, also, that in saying **Our Father**, we express our understanding and acceptance that we, ALL Christians, are part of His family. When we were baptized, we became adopted children of our **Father**.

Petitions: 1–3

1st Petition:

With the words, "Who art in Heaven", Jesus reminds us that our Father is the Supreme Being, King of the Universe, above all things; he, also, reminds us that although we have been baptized into His Royal family, we must remember that He is in Heaven while we continue to toil on earth. We still have much work to do before we can hope to be called Princes and Princesses and share in His Royal Kingdom. Jesus is reminding us that Our Father is infinite and all holy while we are finite and without the holiness necessary to be admitted into His household. His words establish the proper order.

2nd Petition:

Jesus teaches us to say, "hallowed be thy name." Hallow means holy or set apart or to recognize as holy and treat in a holy way. Jesus is instructing us that, in praying, we must hold our Father in the highest regard, offering worship and praise so to honor His **sacred name**.

3rd Petition:

Next, he tells us we are to pray: "thy Kingdom come thy will be done on earth." What did he mean? How can God's Kingdom come to us earthly sinners? What we are praying for, is a share in God's Holiness; that we may receive the graces necessary to live a holy, faith- filled life in accordance with His holy will. In truth, our prayer has already been answered by the coming of Jesus who is, himself, the Kingdom of God. Through his saving **Word** (Holy Scripture) and the sacraments, Jesus, God the Son, has given us the "tools" to grow in holiness with the help of the Holy Spirit. The **OUR FATHER PRAYER** is one of those tools.

Petitions: 4–7

4th Petition:

Jesus tells us to pray, "give us this day our daily bread." Let's break that down: We begin, *Give US*. As children of The Father, we look to Him with lofty expectations as the source of **all** our blessings. Note carefully, Jesus tells us to say, "US" not "ME." In that way, we recognize God as the Father of **all** people and so we pray to Him for the needs (bread) of **all**.

5th Petition:

He instructs us to pray: "Forgive us our trespasses as we forgive those who have hurt us in some way." Note, in this petition we have that little word "**AS**" which couples the two parts of the petition together. That is significant in that with our prayer, we are asking to be forgiven **but**, it is future looking because of the coupling word, **AS**. Accordingly, forgiveness will not be forthcoming if we have not forgiven those who trespass against us.

6th Petition:

Next, we are to pray, "and lead us not into temptation." This line has always given me pause; God is NOT going to LEAD us into temptation. With a little research, I learned that there is a problem with translating the Greek verb "lead" to English. The Greek meaning can be understood as "do not allow us to enter into temptation or, do not let us yield to temptation." Realizing we are constantly doing battle with the evil one in our current culture, we implore our Father, to not allow us to follow the lead of the Devil who represents the way to sin, but to guide our steps in such a way that we avoid the people, places and circumstances where temptation is likely to present itself.

7th Petition:

Finally, Jesus instructs to pray: "but deliver us from evil." Evil has existed since the time of creation and, certainly, Jesus was acutely aware of the evil one since he faced the Devil's temptation in the desert during His forty days sojourn there before beginning his public ministry. Although he failed to sway Jesus, the Devil continues to be ever present in our world today making it more necessary than ever that we continue to seek the help of our Heavenly Father in prayer.

To end this reflection, I want to circle back to Matthew 6:6, where we read these words of Jesus: "when thou prayest, go into thy room and closing the door, pray to thy Father in secret."

Suggested Morning Prayer

Heavenly Father, make me a channel of your perfect love to everyone I meet this day. Amen

14
Judge Not

You may be wondering why I didn't use Jesus' complete statement: "Judge not that you may not be judged."? (Matthew 7:22) I did not because I disagree with the generally accepted interpretation of his words. I understand others can point to the Bible and argue that Jesus was, indeed, instructing his disciples NOT to judge others. I would simply like to suggest we take a closer look at his complete statement, and other sources, to see whether, with additional study, there might be an alternative interpretation. In other words, let's try to see a bigger picture by examining Jesus' statements which preceded Matthew 7:22.

After he was baptized in the Jordan River, Jesus spent the next 40 days in the desert being tempted by the Devil. Upon his return, and learning John the Baptist had been arrested by King Herod, Jesus began his public ministry preaching that the Kingdom of Heaven was at hand and offering a message of a loving and merciful God for those who accepted His Word and repented of their sins, while contrasting it with the Law of Moses under which the Jewish people had lived for many centuries. Jesus taught, "for I say to you that unless your righteousness exceeds that of the Scribes and Pharisees, you shall not enter the Kingdom of Heaven." Further, "I am not here to destroy the law but to fulfill it." (Matthew 5:20)

Now, with that background, let us look at our study passage:

> "Judge not that you be not judged. For with the Judgment you pronounce you will be judged and with the measure you use it will be measured to you. Why do you see the speck that is in your brother's eye but do not notice the log in your own eye? Or, how can you say to your brother, let me take the speck out of your eye when there is a log in your own eye? Thou **hypocrite**, first take the log out of your eye and then you will see clearly to take the speck out of your brother's eye."

I believe Jesus was speaking there about judging in the sense of castigating others or, more precisely, he was referring to finding *fault* in others to cover up one's own faults. It strikes me that the thing here being condemned was the disposition to look unfavorably on the character and/or actions of another which can lead to the uttering of rash, unjust and, perhaps, unkind judgments toward them. I believe that what our Lord was pointing to was the spirit out of which the judgment arose. Now, in reflecting on the last sentence of the passage, I conclude that we are not only *expected* to sit in judgment of our brother's character and actions but, for our own salvation, we are **obligated** to do so if in fact it is our brother's less than acceptable charitable disposition which is being chastised and counseled.

Moreover, I would add that this **obligation** for *holy confrontation* predated Jesus. I discovered this in the Old Testament: God, having appointed the Prophet Ezechiel watchman over the people of Israel, charged him: "therefore thou shalt hear the word from my mouth and shall tell it to them from me. But if **thou tell the wicked man** that he may be converted from his ways and he not be converted from his way, he shall die in his iniquity, but **thou hast delivered thy soul**." (Ezechiel 33:9)

Now also in our passage, we heard Jesus turn things up a notch:

> "Or how will thou say to thy brother, let me remove the speck from thine eye, and behold, a log is in thine eye? THOU HYPOCRITE! First, take the log out of your own eye and then you will see clearly to take the speck out of your brother's eye."

That last statement suggests to me that it is all about **when** and **how** to judge NOT whether to judge at all. Thus, I believe judging is, indeed, necessary! It is but a matter of **judging in the right way at the right time and with the right attitude**.

And, if you need further convincing, consider this: "but if thy brother sin against thee, **go and show him his fault, between you and him alone; if he listens to thee, thou hast won thy brother**." (Matthew 18:15–16)

15

Double Doubts

Our Gospel reading this Sunday was from the Gospel of Mark, Chapter 5:21–43. It is a passage which encased two miracles in one story: the healing of an unnamed woman suffering from hemorrhage for 12 years and the healing of the dying daughter of a synagogue official named Jairus.

Honestly, as I listened to the lector proclaim that reading, I became incredulous; I will explain the reason for my consternation later; however, for this reflection, my goal is to discern the lesson/lessons therein.

As noted in a previous reflection, Mark was most likely the first to write a Gospel describing the WORDS and WORKS of Jesus during his time on earth. He wrote his Gospel in Greek around 50 A.D. I especially like his Gospel because of the details he provides.

Now to our passage, the setting has a large crowd surrounding Jesus. Looking back at Chapter 4, there had been several miracles with large crowds. Even after crossing the Sea of Galilee several times, the crowds always found him.

There are a couple of ways to approach today's story; I chose to focus on the key participants. Of course, we will examine Jesus' words and actions, but the story gets going when our two characters of note enter the picture. Here is the passage, as written:

> *And when Jesus had again crossed over in the boat to the other side, a great crowd gathered together; and he was at the water's edge. And there came one of the rulers of the synagogue named Jairus. And seeing Jesus, he fell at his feet and entreated him much saying, "my daughter is at the point of death; come, lay thy hands upon her that she may be saved and live." And he went away with him, and a great crowd was following him and pressing upon him. And there was a woman who for twelve years had had a hemorrhage and had suffered much at the hands of physicians and had spent all that she had and found no benefit but had rather grew worse. Hearing about Jesus, she came up behind him in the crowd and touched his cloak. For she said, "if I touch but his cloak I shall be saved." And at once the flow of her blood was dried up and she felt in her body that she was healed of her affliction. And Jesus, instantly perceiving in himself that power had gone forth from him, turned to the crowd and said, "who touched my cloak"? And his disciples said to him, "Thou seest the crowd pressing upon thee and dost thou say, who touched me." And he was looking around to see her who had done this. But the woman, fearing and trembling knowing what had happened within her, came, and fell down before him and told him all the truth. But he said to her, "Daughter, thy **faith** has **saved** thee. Go in peace and be thou **healed** of thy affliction." (Mark 5:21-34)*

But wait; there is more:

> *While he was still speaking there came some from the house of the ruler of the synagogue saying. "Thy daughter is dead. Why dost trouble the Master further"? But Jesus having heard what was being said, said to the ruler of the synagogue, "do not be afraid, only have faith." And he allowed no one to follow him except Peter, James, and John, the brother of James. And they came to the house of the ruler of the synagogue, and he saw a tumult of people weeping and wailing greatly. And going in he said to them, "why do you make this din and weep? The girl is asleep, not dead." And they laughed him to scorn. But he, putting them all out, took the father and mother of the girl and those who were with him, and entered in where the girl was lying. And taking the girl by the hand he said to her, "Talitha cumi." which is interpreted, "Girl, I say to you arise." And the girl rose up immediately and began to walk. (Mark 5:25-42)*

Clearly, these two miracle stories speak loudly about the importance of **faith** and **trust** without regard to religious or social status. Also, they speak to the **compassion**, **mercy**, and **healing power** of Jesus.

So, what is it about the story that I find problematic? My issue is with the *narrative* and, specifically with the *two principal characters*, the **unnamed woman**, and a **ruler of the synagogue**, while taking into consideration the Jewish culture at that time. Generally, women had little status; their purpose in life was thought to be providing pleasure and/or offspring to their husbands. They had no social or legal status. With no husband, and no money, this unnamed woman would have been little more than a beggar. The text points out "she heard about Jesus;" so, she was not a follower.

I just do not think that the matter would have unfolded in that way. Then, we heard there was the man in a high religious position, a *ruler of the synagogue*, clearly then, NOT a follower of Jesus, who came, and **fell at the feet** of Jesus. Considering the large mostly Jewish crowd and his high religious position, I believe it would have been MORE than humiliating for him to *FALL* at the feet of Jesus. I must doubt things happened that way.

To me, these are common sense questions. So, having indicated my understanding of the lessons of faith and trust, as well as having noted the compassion, mercy and healing power of Jesus as shown, how does one reconcile these issues of presentation with the Christian view that Holy Scripture is *inspired by God*? With further study and prayer, I found the following to be reassuring:

> *The Gospels are documents of faith. They are the product of faith, and they are intended to call forth faith. Thus, the measure of a Gospel account is the extent of the faith it calls forth and not the accuracy of the narrative details the Gospel author/ authors employed to call forth that faith.*

16

Don't We Need More?

I know in his Gospel at Chapter 21: 21–25, John wrote: "There are many other things Jesus said and did but if every one of these should be written not even the world itself could hold the books that would have to be written." However, would not many of the Gospel stories, although great reading, be even better with additional details? As an example, let us review the passage I chose for this reflection:

Now as Jesus was passing on from there, two blind men followed, crying out, "Son of David, have mercy on us." When Jesus reached the house, the blind men came to him. And Jesus said to them: "Do you believe that I can do this to you"? They answered him: "Yes, Lord." Then he touched their eyes saying: "Let it be done to you according to your faith." And their eyes were opened. And Jesus strictly charged them saying: "See that no one knows of this." But they went out and spread his fame abroad throughout all that district. (Matthew 9: 27–31)

First, this story is found ONLY in Matthew's Gospel which always makes me curious; but, beyond that, it is lacking so much detail that it seems to detract from the overall beauty of the event. Here is what I mean:

"Two blind men followed."

How can **blind men follow**?

Did the disciples lead them? Friends?

"When he had reached the house, the blind men came to him." Did he enter the house? If so, who all was there? How could "they come to him?"

And Jesus *strictly charged them saying*: "**See that no one knows of this**." But they went out and spread his fame throughout the whole district. Of course, they did! Going from being blind to being able to see; their life changed completely; who wouldn't want to tell the world?

So, yes, **I thought I needed to know more**; at least as to why and when they became blind; but I ultimately realized that packed into those eight short lines, is a wonderful story about **HOPE**. Needing background, I found Luke's Gospel to be most informative; his chapter 9 begins: Jesus was in Capharnaum. "Now as Jesus passed on from there." (Matthew 9:9) And if we then look at Mark's Gospel we read, "And when Jesus had again crossed over in the boat to the other side *a great crowd followed him.* (Mark 5:21) and again, "And he went away with him and *a great crowd was following him.* (Mark 5:24) Finally, "Thou seest the *crowd* pressing upon thee… (Mark 5:31) So these two blind men, presumably led by someone, **fought the crowds** to pursue Jesus. Their **FAITH** gave them **HOPE** and kept them pressing forward.

FINALLY, they caught up with Jesus and cried out "**Son of David** have mercy on us." Jesus said to them, "Do you believe that I can do this to you?" They answered, "**yes LORD**."

These men were *true disciples*; they knew Jesus well—"Son of David" AND addressed him as *LORD* in answering his question, "do you believe?"

"Let it be done to you ACCORDING TO YOUR FAITH."

Lesson 1:

This miracle, of course, should teach us the value of *relentlessly* pursuing Jesus regardless of what obstacles (blindness or crowds) are in our path. Never lose hope! Never give up. PRAY! Continue to FOLLOW the PATH to Jesus.

Lesson 2:

Don't do as I did: When you focus too much on details, you risk missing the big picture.

17

The Greatest Parable

Let us begin this reflection by again defining the word parable: A parable is a short story that uses comparison, symbolism, or analogy to illustrate a moral lesson, a religious principle, or a universal truth.

As noted in an earlier reflection, the Synoptic Gospels tell us that Jesus utilized the teaching "tool" of "parable" 39–50 times. Of those, the Parable of the Sower is the most meaningful to me, personally, because of its agricultural reference with which I can relate having been raised on a farm.

It is described in all three Synoptic Gospels, albeit with differences which I will get into later in this study. For our review, we will use Matthew's version of the story.

As I frequently do, I will backtrack in Matthew and look at the setting for this event before we get into the passage itself. In Chapters 11 and 12 we saw Jesus, seemingly, getting frustrated with the Jewish people in the crowds either because they were not accepting his teaching about the Kingdom of God or didn't understand it. Consequently, now in Chapter 13, we find that Jesus launched into a series of parables which make up the entire Chapter; The Parable of the Sower begins that series:

And he spoke to them many things in parables, saying: "Behold, the sower went out to sow. And as he sowed, some seeds fell by the wayside and the birds came and ate them up. And other seeds fell upon rocky ground where they had not much earth; it sprang up quickly but when the sun came up the plants were scorched and withered because they had no roots. And other seeds fell among the thorns and the thorns grew up and choked them. And other seeds fell upon good ground and yielded fruit, some a hundredfold, some sixtyfold and some thirtyfold. He who has ears; let him hear. (Matthew 13:1–23)

It is easy to identify God, the Father, as the sower in this passage and to praise His **generosity**; He offers His blessings (seed) to everyone without exception. As we read in Matthew 5:45: "God lets his sun shine on the bad and the good." It is also likely that Jesus intended his listeners (and us) to see themselves/ourselves as the **soil**, the recipients of his seed. Therefore, the questions he put before them were: "What is the condition of your heart? Will my seed (Word) take root and thrive or suffer the consequences of falling on the path, on rocky soil or among thorns"?

Some students of the Bible have made much of Jesus' reference to production; in Matthew's Gospel, he said it produced one hundredfold, sixtyfold, or thirtyfold; in Mark's thirty, sixty and one hundred and in Luke's, simply one hundred. While that might be significant to some, to me, it is meaningless except to suggest that Jesus' listeners, many of them farmers, could equate those numbers to a bountiful harvest—a good return for their hard work. I feel even more meaningful than the production aspect, is Jesus' subsequent comment: "for him who has shall be given and he shall have abundance; but from him who does not have, even that which he has shall be taken away." My conclusion is that in this parable the **seed** is the **gift of faith**. Yes, indeed! Unless we *cultivate* the **grace of faith**, we may lose it due to the many distractions and/or temptations we encounter in our world today. So, whether we see God's **seed**, spoken of by Jesus, as the **grace of faith** or **His Holy Word** we MUST ACT in order for that **seed** to be productive. But don't just take my word, listen to Jesus: "one who hears my words **but does not put them into practice** is like a man who built his house without a foundation; the floods (temptation) came, and the house collapsed (sin) into ruin." (Luke 6: 49)

MAY YOU ENJOY A BOUNTIFUL HARVEST!

18

Parable of the Mustard Seed

Although one of the shortest of the parables used by Jesus in his teaching, it is one of the most studied and discussed.

To me, one of the indications of the significance of any parable is whether it is included in more than one of the Synoptic Gospels; this one is described, albeit with differences, in all three. As indicated previously, John's Gospel does not include any parables.

For this reflection, we will follow Matthew's version; that seems appropriate since his Gospel contains 20 parables, many more than the other authors. In addition, this parable is one of seven which Matthew clustered in Chapter 13; and I believe some of those are interrelated.

Just a reminder, a parable, by definition, is a simple story told by Jesus to illustrate a moral or spiritual lesson.

The Parable of the Mustard Seed:

> *Another parable he set before them saying, "The kingdom of heaven is like a grain of mustard seed which a man took and sowed in his field. This indeed is the smallest of all the seeds; but when it grows up it is larger than any herb and becomes a tree, so that the birds of the air come and dwell in its branches." (Matthew 13:31–32)*

It should be noted that this parable is the third parable of the seven in Chapter 13; and in each of those three Jesus speaks of seeds being sown. It seems likely that Jesus recognized that he was speaking to a mostly agriculture familiar crowd. In parable number one, Jesus suggests that God, the Father, is the Sower who sows (grants) seed (faith); and he talks about the problems with the seed (faith) surviving because of evil (rocks, thorns etc.) In parable number two, he suggests that the Devil will try to disrupt the growth of the seed (faith) in which it has taken root by sowing opportunities for sin (weeds). In number three, Jesus speaks of the POTENTIAL for the KINGDOM of HEAVEN on Earth from a single seed (God's Word) growing into a huge plant (church) where birds (all believers) can dwell (find salvation).

The early fathers of the church suggested thus: Christ himself is the grain of mustard seed, who planted in the garden of the sepulcher grew up a great tree; he was a grain of seed when he died, and a tree when he rose again; a grain of seed in the humiliation of the flesh, a tree in the power of his majesty.

Another school of thought I uncovered suggests that the *seed* is the Word sown by God as the Sower; and likewise, in our passage today, the mustard seed is the Word of God which, when planted in a field, (believers) has the potential to become a tree (the church) where birds, all birds, can find a fit dwelling place. That line of thinking would suggest the Gentiles, as being the birds finding the kingdom of heaven therein.

Personally, I have a different thought on the *birds*; I believe Jesus was depicting them as the *Devil* who is always around trying to interfere with the intended message of the Word. In the "Sower" parable the *birds* ate the Word (seed). In the Parable of the Mustard Seed, they came and stayed (dwelled) in the *branches* so as to be ever present to tempt Christian believers into sin and interfere with Christ's stated goal that there be but **ONE CHURCH**.

But wait, Jesus concluded the parable of The Mustard Seed with these words: "The kingdom of heaven is like leaven which a woman took and **buried** in three measures of flour, until all of it was leavened." What is that all about? I submit Jesus was saying that with the Mustard Tree, he had established his kingdom of heaven on Earth – the church. At that time, however, his word was buried under the flour of ignorance. i.e., refusal or inability to understand. In time, his leaven (Word) would rise and flourish due to the understanding and preaching of the apostles. God's plan for salvation at work!

Finally, our challenge is to listen to the parables as proclaimed in church and/or read and reflect on them, in private, to try to discern Jesus' teaching. Thankfully, there is no right or wrong interpretation; what matters most is that we are spending time with Jesus' Word, trying to uncover his message and, by virtue of our effort, draw closer to him.

19

Keep Searching

That title hints at my struggle to understand the Miracle of the Loaves and Fishes.

As I mentioned previously, Jesus performed 37 miracles during his time on Earth. Since I have been following his trail with these reflections, so far, I have studied and reflected on seven of those events. As I read those passages as described in one or more of the Gospels, I tried to imagine what took place there as if it might be portrayed in a movie. That was relatively easy as I envisioned Jesus changing water into wine, or healing someone, or restoring sight to a blind man or even raising a person from the dead. But how does one visualize, seemingly out of thin air, enough barley loaves to feed five thousand and still have twelve basketfuls left over? I could not so we will try a different tact; What was Jesus up to? Why did he do what he did, at that time and in that place? Hopefully, we can find some answers in this passage from John's Gospel:

> *Now the Passover, the feast of the Jews was near, when, therefore, Jesus had lifted his eyes and seeing that a very great crowd had come to him he said to Philip: "Whence shall we buy **bread** that these may eat?" But he said this to try him for he himself knew what he would do. Andrew, the brother of Simon Peter said to him, "there is a young boy here who has **five barley loave**s and two fishes; but what are these among so many?" Jesus said, "make the people recline." Now there was much grass in the place. The men therefore reclined, in number **about five thousand**. Jesus then took the **loaves and when he had given thanks** distributed them to those reclining; and likewise, the fishes, as much as they wished. But when they were filled, he said to the disciples, "Gather the fragments that are left over lest they be wasted." They therefore gathered them up and they filled twelve baskets. (John 6:4–13)*

Some Scripture scholars suggest looking for ties to the Old Testament; indeed, Jesus, throughout his ministry, often referred to the Old Testament. We will do that but first, these lines in the passage sent me searching for the **meaning** of this **miracle**:

- Now the Passover, the feast of the Jews was near.

- When therefore, Jesus had lifted up his eyes and seen a very great **crowd**.

- But he said this to try him for he himself knew what he would do.

- A young boy here who has **five barley loaves** and two fishes.

- When he had given thanks, he **distributed** them to those reclining.

Next, let's look to the Old Testament to help us understand Jesus' actions:

- "I will raise them up a prophet out of their midst of their brethren like to thee. And I will put my words in his mouth, and he shall speak to them all that I shall command him." (Deuteronomy 18:18)

- Behold the Lord God shall come with strength and his arm shall *rule*. Behold his reward is with him and his work is before him. He shall **feed his flock** like a shepherd. (Isaiah 40:10–11)

- And a certain man came from Baalsalisa bringing to **man of God bread of the first fruits, twenty loaves of barley**. (Kings 4:42–44)

- Why do you spend money for that which is not **bread** and your labor for that which doth not satisfy you? (Isaiah 55:2)

Observations and Conclusions

Careful reading shows great symbolism: First crowd/flock. Barley loaves/Baalsalia from the Old Testament. The number five depicts the Five Books of Moses. The number twelve, of course, being the number of the apostles. Finally, "he distributed them" / "he shall feed his flock." (Note: All three of the Synoptic Gospel authors wrote, "he *broke the loaves* and gave them to the apostles to give to the crowd.")

The Miracle of the **Loaves** and **Fishes** points backwards to words and events in the Old Testament to give us clues as to who Jesus really is and, also, points us forward to what Jesus will do in the Upper Room on the night before he died.

20

Don't Give Up. Don't Ever Give Up!

Our Gospel reading for this Sunday from the Gospel of Matthew, Chapter 15:21–28 brought to my mind those famous words spoken in 1993 by the then men's basketball coach at NC State, Jim Valvano, as he fought the final weeks of his fight against terminal cancer. In today's passage, we heard about an exchange between Jesus and a Canaanite woman.

Before we begin our study of the event described in that passage, I think it would be good to add a little background for context; Jesus was well into his earthly ministry, having worked numerous miracles and was attracting great crowds everywhere he went. His enormous popularity did not go unnoticed by the Jewish religious leaders who felt threatened and were watching him closely seeking to find something to hold against him. Then, they came to him saying, "Why do thy disciples transgress the tradition of the ancients? For they do not wash their hands when they take food." Jesus then delivered one of his most profound statements:

"Hear and understand. What goes into the mouth does not defile a man; but it is what comes out of his mouth that defiles a man."

Then, Matthew, beginning at verse 21 describes today's Gospel story:

> *And leaving there, Jesus retired to the district of Tyre and Sidon. And behold a Canaanite woman came out of that territory and cried out to him, saying,* **"Have pity on me, O Lord, Son of David! My daughter is sorely beset by a devil."** *He answered her not a word. And his disciples came up and besought him saying: "Send her away, for she is crying out after us."*

Perhaps, we should look more closely at what was going on here with the disciples; any woman, not just this woman, would be shunned because in their Jewish society women had no legal and no social standing. Moreover, since she was a Gentile, the Jewish disciples would consider her not only unsaved (they considered themselves saved) but unworthy of salvation.

> **He answered her not a word!** *Then,* **"I was not sent except to the lost sheep of the house of Israel."**

> *But she came and* **worshipped him**! *Saying:* **"Lord, help me."**

> *He said in answer: "It is not fair to take the children's bread and to cast it to the dogs." But she said," Yes,* **Lord**; *for even the dogs eat of the* **crumbs that fall from their Master's Table**.*"*

> *Then Jesus answered and said to her: "Oh woman, great is thy* **Faith**! *Let it be* **Done** *to thee as thou wilt." And her daughter was healed from that moment!*

This is a wonderful story about faith and prayer; I especially enjoyed the dialogue between Jesus and this Gentile woman; words worthy of reflection!

- Woman: "Have pity on me, Oh Lord, Son of David My daughter is sorely beset by a devil."

    By addressing Jesus as *Lord*, we know she was a believer recognizing Jesus as God and Savior although she was not a disciple. Note as well, her reference to *Son of David* indicating she was, also, knowledgeable about Jesus' heritage as well as the Old Testament.

- Jesus: "I was not sent except to the lost sheep of the house of Israel."

    At this point in time, he was focused on his mission to change the hearts and minds of the Jewish people.

- Woman: She came and *worshipped him* saying, "Lord, help me."

    Her prayer: she first gave humble praise and then **persisted**.

- Jesus: "It is not fair to take the children's bread and cast it to the dogs."

    He reminds the woman you are a Gentile and not of the house of Israel.

- Woman: "Yes, Lord; for even the dogs eat of the crumbs that fall from their master's table.

    She acknowledges and respects Jesus' earthly mission, as stated, but has **faith and trust in God's infinite love and mercy**.

Jesus:

> "O woman, great is your faith! Let it be done to thee as thou wilt."

This story offers us a great lesson on the need to persist in our prayers. In addition, we have this from Jesus:

> Suppose one of you goes to his friend house at midnight and says, "Friend, lend me three loaves of bread, because a friend of mine has come to me on a journey and I have nothing to set before him." And the one inside answers, "Do not bother me. My door is already shut, and my children are with me in bed. I cannot get up to give you anything." I tell you, even though he will not get up to provide for him because of his friendship, yet because of the man's **persistence** he will get up and give him as much as he needs (Luke 11: 5–8)

Lesson on Prayer: DON'T GIVE UP! DON'T EVER GIVE UP!

21

Sometimes I Wonder

Our Gospel reading last Sunday described yet another occasion where Jesus healed a blind man. As the story was proclaimed, something seemed a little strange and left me wondering.

That passage was from the Gospel of Mark, Chapter 8:22–26:

> *And they came to Bethsaida, and they brought him a blind man and entreated him to touch him. And, taking the blind man by the hand, he led him forth outside the village; and applying spittle to his eyes, he laid his hands upon him and asked him if he saw anything; and the man looked up and said, "I see men as though they were trees, but walking about." Then, again, he laid his hand upon the man's eyes, and he began to see and was restored so that he saw all things plainly. And he sent him to his house saying, "go to thy house and if thou enter the village, tell nobody."*

Now, I wonder, who were the "they" who brought the blind man to Jesus? I wonder why he led the blind man away from the village before healing him? I wonder why it took two attempts for Jesus to heal the man? Finally, I wonder why this event is described only in Mark's Gospel? Even the other two Synoptic Gospel authors did not include it in their Gospels.

Since Mark's Gospel is regarded as the most "historical" of the gospels, preserving the most accurate order of events albeit lacking some detail, I decided I would look more closely at his description of this miracle.

However, before we dig deeper into our passage, I feel some background information might be helpful: The village in the story is Bethsaida, which lays on the northeast shore of the Sea of Galilee. It is significant to our story in that Bethsaida was the site of several of Jesus' miracles. Unfortunately, by the time Jesus left the area to continue his journey to Jerusalem his Word had not been well understood or accepted by those villagers. (Matthew 11:21)

Just a brief reminder, at that time, blindness was considered evidence of sin of the afflicted person or his parents. Thus, this blind man who was brought to Jesus would have been considered a sinner, an outcast and, most likely, was a beggar.

And, finally, which I have learned from experience, a little extra reading of Scripture can be helpful as well; so, at the beginning of Mark's Chapter 8 we find where Jesus fed four thousand people with just seven loaves. (Mark 8:1–9) That event was followed by the Pharisees demanding a sign, even though they had just watched Jesus miraculously feed the four thousand. (MK 8:10–12) Jesus' day then worsened when his apostles, who also had witnessed the feeding as well as the Pharisee dust-up, didn't understand the significance of that miracle, prompting Jesus to exclaim, seemingly, in dismay, "Is your heart still *blinded*? Though you have eyes to **see** do you not **see**?" (Mark 8:18)

I think that background offers a good lead-in to today's passage. Clearly, there were ill feelings between Jesus and those non-Christian Jewish villagers. He even began to reproach the towns in which most of his miracles had been worked, because they had not repented, "Woe to thee Bethsaida." (Matthew 12:20–21)

And, as indicated, the Jewish religious leaders were increasingly a challenge to Jesus, as they diligently searched for ways to trap him with the goal of having him arrested. I strongly suspect it was some of those non-believing villagers who brought this blind man to Jesus to try to somehow trap him. While, recognizing their **hypocrisy**, nonetheless, Jesus felt **pity** for the blind man. So, he took him out of their sight for the healing. That disdain for them would also explain his instruction to the man to "go to thou house."

Now to address the remaining "wonder": why Jesus used two attempts to heal the man. Keeping in mind that Mark's source was very likely Peter, I believe Mark was drawing a parallel between the man *not seeing clearly* after just one attempt and Jesus' statement to the apostles when they did not understand after they witnessed the miracle of his feeding four thousand: "Though you have eyes to see do you not see?" Similarly, I suspect the reason the other authors chose *not* to *include the event* was because of the two attempts to heal; they, perhaps, sensed their individual communities of recent converts would not understand.

22

The Doctrine of the Cross

The title is a quote from page 71 of the New Testament; it is taken from Luke's Gospel. The passage that follows is quite short, but one I found to be very meaningful and certainly worthy of reflection.

As usual, I believe some background information will be helpful. Jesus is nearing the end of his missionary journey from the Jordan River to Jerusalem. Having just fed five thousand with five loaves and two fishes, he and his disciples went off to pray. It was then that he instructed them: "The Son of Man must suffer many things and be rejected by the elders and chief priests and Scribes and be put to death and on the third day rise again." It is at this point we read this brief, but inspiring passage:

> And he said to **all**, "If **anyone** wishes to come after me, let him **deny himself** and **take up his cross** daily and **follow me**. For he who would **save his life** will

*lose it; but he who **loses his life** for my sake will **save it**." (Luke 9:23–24)*

Considerations:

- First, notice Jesus extended his *invitation* to **all**; he did not limit it to his disciples or those who had accepted his teachings. Note, even non-believers were NOT excluded!

- Second, "let him **deny himself**." These are confounding words; what does it mean to deny *HIMSELF*? I do not think Jesus was referring to our denying ourselves of the pleasures we now have; I believe there is a much deeper meaning. I submit each of us has a *true* self; it is mine and mine alone. To "come after Jesus" requires that we *GIVE* that self to him. Subsequently, we will no longer be burdened by our previously *self-imposed* measures of success or failures; we will be free to **follow him**; to seek only his will.

- Next, "**take up his cross daily**." No, Jesus was not speaking about the crosses of pain, in all its forms, which we may face each day. Neither was he speaking about the strength or toughness we currently need to manage our perceived hardships each day. I believe "taking up our cross" means we must *overcome our human tendency to consider ME FIRST* and fully embrace his teaching of LOVE GOD and LOVE OF NEIGHBOR. Then there is that little word "daily." Jesus is telling us, there, that to be "a follower" requires us to change who we have been by making a "daily" effort to die to ourselves and our selfish desires.

- "He who would **save HIS life** will lose it." For sure, Jesus was not referring to **his life** as in his physical life; rather I would suggest he had in mind a *life of sin* and its effect on salvation. Should one choose to continue his sinful ways he will lose his **spiritual life**. Instead, should one surrender his sinful ways for the sake of the Gospel, Jesus says that man will **save his life** and have eternal life.

Finally, Jesus knew this "charge" to his disciples and **ALL**, which includes us, would be exceedingly difficult so he left them and us with these words in John 14: 1–4, 15–16, 18:

> *Let not your heart be troubled. You believe in God, believe also in me. In my father's house there are many mansions. Were it not so, I should have told you because I go and **prepare a place for you**. And if I go to prepare a place for you, I am coming again, and I will take you to myself; that where I am there you also may be.*

> *If you love me, keep my commandments. And I will ask the Father and he will give you another Advocate to dwell with you forever.*

> *I will not leave you orphans; I will come to you.*

A lot to think about for sure.

23

The Transfiguration

This week's Sunday liturgy included a reading on The Transfiguration of Jesus as described in the Gospel of Luke. As a matter of interest, the *event* is described in all three Synoptic Gospels.

Although it is a fascinating story, bible scholars have hesitated to try to explain, not just the event itself, but the reason it took place at all. Without regard to their reluctance, I will offer my thoughts.

The Transfiguration is considered one of the five milestones of Jesus' earthly ministry. The other four being his Baptism, Crucifixion, Resurrection and Ascension.

A quick look at Webster's dictionary was of no help: Transfiguration—the act of being transfigured. Research turned up a better definition: The *Transfiguration* is the outward manifestation of the inner person as revealed by God.

To proceed, let us read the passage as it was proclaimed:

Now it came to pass about eight days after these words, that he took Peter, James and John and went up the mountain to pray. And, as he prayed, the appearance of his countenance was changed, and his raiment became a radiant white. And behold, two men were talking with him. And these were Moses and Elias, who appearing in glory, spoke of his death, which he was about to fulfill in Jerusalem.

Now Peter and his companions were heavy with sleep. But when they were fully awake, they saw his glory and the two men standing with him. And it came to pass, as they were parting from him, that Peter said to Jesus, "Master, it is good for us to be here. And let us set up three tents, one for thee, one for Moses and one for Elias." Not knowing what he said. But, as he was done speaking thus, there came a cloud and overshadowed them; and they were afraid when they entered the cloud. And there came a voice out of the cloud saying: "This is my beloved Son, hear him." And after the voice had passed, Jesus was found alone. And they kept silence and told no one at that time any of these things they had seen. (Luke 9:28–36)

As noted, The Transfiguration is included in all three Synoptic Gospels, but with differences. I used Luke's version here since it was his Gospel which was proclaimed. In my study I noted he included few references to the Old Testament. Matthew, on the other hand, often cited the Old Testament since he was writing for early Jewish Christian converts and his loyal followers. Luke wrote for a more Gentile audience.

Interestingly, biblical scholars have opined that Mark was the first to pen a Gospel and both Matthew and Luke borrowed generously from his effort.

At this point, perhaps it would be worthwhile to touch on some of the similarities and differences in those Gospels. An area of agreement was at the beginning of all three gospels, where the authors noted the event took place on a **mountain**. In those days, it was believed that a mountain was the meeting point between heaven and earth. Moreover, mountains were seen as a **setting for Divine experiences**. On the other hand, one area of difference was Jesus' appearance: Mark, while noting Jesus was transfigured, then said "and his *clothes became dazzling white, such as no one on earth could bleach them."* Matthew took it a step further: *"And his face shone as the sun and his garments became white as snow."* A *second area of difference* was related to time; you will recall Luke began: "Now it came to pass about eight days after these words." Per Matthew: "Now after six days."

To me the difference between six and eight days is of little importance. What is important is WHY; WHY The Transfiguration took place at all, especially at that point in Jesus' ministry. Previously, in Luke there were several familiar stories, including the Parable of the Sower, the healing of the woman with longstanding hemorrhaging and the feeding of the five thousand with just a few loaves and fishes. THEN came the passage titled, "Peter's Confession." It was then that Jesus asked his *apostles*, "who do the crowds say that I am," and then, "who do you say I am"? Seemingly, only Peter answered correctly. That verbal exchange is *then* followed by the **Transfiguration**. While the timing is curious, a more critical concern for me has to do with the relationship between "Peter's Confession" and The Transfiguration.

So, I turned to Mark's Gospel and in Chapter 8 came upon the story of the "loaves and fishes." Also of significance, I believe, is this next passage In Mark's Gospel which Luke failed to even mention: And he left them and getting into the boat crossed the sea. And they had forgotten to bring bread. And they began to argue among themselves saying, "we have no bread." But Jesus knowing this, said to them: "Why do you argue because you have no bread? **Do you not yet perceive, nor understand? Is your heart still blinded? Though you have eyes, do you not see, and though you have ears do you not hear?**" (Mark 8:13–18) One can, almost, sense the disappointment and frustration in Jesus' words. Clearly, the apostles were greatly lacking in their ability to understand Jesus' teaching on the Kingdom of God and his role in the Father's plan of salvation.

Because of the oddity of *where* The Transfiguration is found in Holy Scripture and considering the above verses, I submit that Jesus realized the Apostles were not ready for his death on the cross, his Resurrection and his planned role for them in his Church thereafter; thus he prevailed on the Father and Holy Spirit to give them increased grace for understanding his message of love of God and love of neighbor. And, of course, we know the Father heard his plea; recall His words: "**this is my beloved son, HEAR HIM.**" Did they?

Thank God for Pentecost!

24
Choices

This reflection looks at a somewhat unique story about Jesus visiting the home of two women, Martha and Mary; it is offered only in Luke's Gospel. Seemingly, Luke, as opposed to the other two Synoptic Gospel authors, Matthew, and Mark, utilizes women in contrast to the social stature women held among pagans and Jews at that time.

The setting finds Jesus continuing his travels having set a lawyer straight on the question of how one must act to gain eternal life with the Parable of the Good Samaritan:

> *Now it came to pass as they were on their journey, that he entered a certain village; and a woman named Martha welcomed him to her house. And she had a sister called Mary, who also seated herself at the Lord's feet, and listened to his word. But Martha was busy about much serving. And she came up and said: "Lord, is it no concern of thine that my sister has*

*left me to serve alone? Tell her therefore to help me."
But he answered and said to her: "Martha, Martha,
thou art anxious and troubled about many things;
and yet only one thing is needful. Mary has chosen
the best part, and it will not be taken away from her."*
(Luke 10:38–42)

Before we take a closer look at the "choice" each of the women made, I would point out that in that culture *hospitality* toward an arriving guest was especially important. So, let's not be too hard on Martha. Was Jesus not familiar with the custom? It would seem he was tough on Martha, as indicated by his using her name twice in his admonishment, even given that he clearly had the authority to do so.

I would suggest that Jesus would rather we focus on the key words in the passage: **"only one thing is needful."** Here, he was sending a message to Martha, AND to us. Jesus is well aware of each of our day-to-day obligations as well as the unending distractions which abound. He wishes to encourage us to NOT LOSE SIGHT of the importance of spending time with him and, especially, **HIS WORD**. I'm quite sure, that on this day, he is pleased that *you have chosen the better part*.

25
Faith: How Much is Enough?

For our study today we will be reflecting on a passage from Matthew's Gospel. On first reading, it seemed to be a simple story of Jesus healing a young boy who was possessed by an evil spirit such that he would fall into a fire. After some thought, I decided there is one other aspect of the story that is worthy of another look.

It should be noted that this event followed The Transfiguration where Peter, James and John accompanied Jesus up the mountain for that wonderous event.

This is Matthew 17:14–20:

> And when he had come to the crowd, a man approached him and threw himself on his knees before him, saying, "Lord, have pity on my son for he is a lunatic and suffers severely; for often he falls into a fire and often into the water. And I brought him to

thy disciples; but they could not cure him." Jesus answered and said, "O unbelieving and perverse generation. How long shall I be with you? How long shall I put up with you"? "Bring him here to me." And Jesus rebuked him; and the devil went out of him and from that moment the boy was cured.

Just a quick reminder; In the reflection on The Transfiguration, we looked at prior stories where Jesus expressed dismay with the apostles because of their **lack of understanding** even after following him for many months and listening to his teachings. In this story he *seems* to be somewhat annoyed by their **lack of faith**, given what we read in Matthew 10: Jesus called unto himself the twelve disciples and gave the power over **unclean** spirits. And the disciples were confused and came to Jesus privately and said, "Why could not we cast it out"? He said to them, "Because of your little faith; for amen I say to you if you have faith like a mustard seed you will say to this mountain, 'Remove from here;' and it will remove. And nothing will be impossible to you. But this **kind** can be cast out only by prayer and fasting."

Interestingly, Mark, in his Gospel, wrote about the event a little differently; there the father of the boy beseeched Jesus after the disciples were unable to heal the boy. Note the father's words to Jesus, "help us **if you can**." In Mark, Jesus chastises the father for insufficient faith. But the key point of that passage is summed up with these words, "anything is possible IF you have sufficient faith." (Mark 9:22)

Finally, we need to clear up any remaining confusion because of these words: "Oh unbelieving and perverse generation. How long shall I be with you? How long shall I put up with you?" Some have concluded Jesus was again castigating his disciples; I think not. I submit Jesus was addressing those words to a "faith-less crowd", as well as the father of the boy. But the boy was ultimately healed when the father offered this prayer to Jesus, "Lord, **help my unbelief**!"

If you remember nothing else about this story, remember:

ANYTHING IS POSSIBLE IF YOU HAVE SUFFICIENT FAITH

and

JESUS HEARS THE HUMBLE PRAYER

26

Winners and Loser

As I was reading Luke's Gospel, a passage got my attention prompting me to take a closer look. I found it to be more than just a story about one of the 23 healing miracles Jesus worked during his time on Earth.

As noted previously, at that time, it was felt that any affliction, such as we have here, physical, mental, or emotional was *caused* by *sin* committed by the afflicted person or his/her parent.

With that said, I believe it would be best to quote the passage rather than to paraphrase it:

> *Now he was teaching in one of their synagogues on the Sabbath. And behold, there was a woman who for eighteen years had had a sickness caused by a spirit; and she was bent over and utterly unable to look upward. When Jesus saw her, he called her to him and said to her, "Woman, thou are delivered from thy infirmity." And he laid his hands upon her, and instantly she was made straight and glorified God.*

> *But the ruler of the synagogue, indignant that Jesus had cured on the Sabbath, addressed the crowd, saying, "There are six days in which one ought to work; on these therefore come and be cured, not on the Sabbath" But the Lord answered him and said, "Hypocrites! Does not each one of you on the Sabbath loose his ox or ass from the manger, and lead it forth to water? And this woman, daughter of Abraham as she is, whom Satan has bound, lo for eighteen years, ought not she be loosed from this bond on the Sabbath"? And as he said these things, all his adversaries were put to shame; and the entire crowd rejoiced at all the glorious things done by him. (Luke 13:10–17)*

At first blush, this seems like an event where a compassionate Jesus heals a woman who had suffered with an affliction for a long time. However, he did so on the *Sabbath*, which was forbidden by Mosaic Law, resulting in a "testy" verbal exchange between Jesus and ruler of the synagogue. Of course, Jesus won that verbal battle such that the ruler of the synagogue was "put to shame."

Now, let us go through the event step by step or, word for word, if you will, focusing on the key participants: Jesus, the woman, and the ruler.

> Jesus sees the afflicted woman in the synagogue and *calls her to him*.
> The suffering woman was a *person of faith* being in the synagogue.
> The woman said not a word before she was cured.
> The "healing" took place on the Sabbath in violation of Mosaic Law.
> The ruler of the synagogue said to the crowd *that it was against the law*. Jesus shamed the ruler by using an easily understood argument.

WINNERS: Jesus and the woman
LOSER: The ruler of the synagogue

That could be considered the end of the story; however, I think that there is more to this passage; I believe there is another aspect that needs to be explored. Given the statements of the ruler of the synagogue to the *crowd* that **healing** is not to be done on the **Sabbath** and Jesus' retort, "**Hypocrites**" pointing out *folks don't just rest on the Sabbath*, they DO WHATEVER HAS TO BE DONE, a question entered my mind: What role should the "Sabbath" play in our lives"? Should we be guided by the Torah and one of its 613 laws calling for *REST* and providing legal consequences for "work" or can we spend time with God in worship, private prayer etc. AND interact with our neighbor, doing good?

Keep in mind the genesis of the Sabbath (rest) was God with the completion of creation; on the seventh day He rested. Yes, AND then He interacted with all that He had made and saw that it was good.

It comes down to the word—WORK. In Deuteronomy 5:12–15, Moses in handing down the ten commandments, and referring to the seventh day declared, "Thou shall not do any work therein." The Mosaic Law, later changed that to where even *words of healing with laying on of hands* was "work" and a violation of the law. Jesus, quite deftly, set that record straight.

Remember: "The Sabbath was made for man and not man for the Sabbath." (Mark 2:27)

27
The Question

For this reflection we will continue with the Gospel according to Luke. You might recall, our previous reflection looked at the story of Jesus, while teaching in their synagogue on the Sabbath, healed a woman who had been afflicted with a sickness which caused her to be bent over such that she could not look up. (Luke 13:10–17)

Today, with our passage, we will study some important questions, and I believe we need to read it completely:

> *And he passed on through towns and villages, teaching and making his way toward Jerusalem. But someone said to him, "Lord, **are only a few to be saved?**" But he said to them, "Strive to enter by the narrow gate; for many, I tell you, will seek to enter but will not be able. But when the master of the house has entered and shut the door, you will begin to stand outside and knock at the door saying, "Lord, open for*

> us." And he shall say to you in answer, "I do not know where you are from." Then you shall begin to say, "we ate and drank in thy presence, and thou didst teach in our streets." And he shall say to you, "I do not know where you are from. Depart from me all you workers of iniquity. There will be weeping and gnashing of teeth when you shall see Abraham and Isaac and Jacob and all the Prophets in the kingdom of God, but you yourselves cast forth outside; and, they shall come from the east and from the west; from the north and from the south, and will feast in the kingdom of God; and, behold, there are **those last who will be first** and there are **those first who will be last**." (Luke 13:23–35)

Again, you will recall in Luke 13:10–17 that a ruler of the synagogue challenged Jesus for *healing on the Sabbath* saying it was illegal under Mosaic Law, prompting Jesus to call those Jewish religious leaders hypocrites.

Now, with that backdrop, I will point out that **Jesus did not answer the question of how many will be saved**. Many have speculated on an answer; they do not know. Neither do I. In fact, I suggest Jesus did not answer the question directly because **he also did not know**.

Before offering support for that last statement, let us look more closely at the overall situation. The questioner was, in all likelihood, a Jewish protagonist who would have been knowledgeable in Jewish history prompting Jesus to reference prominent figures from the Old Testament in his response; and, with these words, he went on to remind the Jews that they had failed to honor their original **covenant with God**: "When the Master has risen *locked the door then shall* **YOU** stand outside *knocking and* *saying," Lord, open for us."* And he will say to you in answer, **"I do not know where you are from."**

Of additional importance, I believe, is that Jesus' remarks were clearly aimed at the Jewish religious leaders and cast in the future tense: "You **will** begin to stand outside and knock at the door." And the last line says: "And behold, there are those last who **will** be first and those first who **will** be last." Those words suggest to me the **ANSWER** will come on judgment day.

So now, let us look more closely at a couple more verbal exchanges and a suggested meaning:

They said, "You taught in our streets."

Jesus says, "I don't know where you are from."

TRANSLATION: Does not matter which religion you belong to.

They said, "We ate and drank in your presence."

Jesus says, "I don't know where you are from."

TRANSLATION: Sure, you are here in church, BUT what have you done **outside of these walls** to live out my command to love your neighbor as yourself?

To circle back, Jesus *did not answer the question of whether only a few would be saved* because he didn't know; the reason being— **MAN'S FREE WILL**.

That leaves us with one unanswered question: What exactly did Jesus mean by using the words—*narrow gate*? My thought there is that Jesus was telling those Jewish listeners that they should understand that they had forfeited their priority status so now they were in line with everyone else, people from all directions.

We, too, are subject to the narrow gate test. In other Scripture passages we get a sense of what His words entail: "go sell whatever thou hast and give to the poor. And thou shalt have treasure in heaven; and come follow me. (Mark 10:21)

Or "none, having put his hand to the plow and *looking back* is fit for the Kingdom of God." (Luke 9:62)

And, finally, consider this: "If anyone comes to me and does not hate his own father and mother and wife and children and brother and sister, yes, even his own life, cannot be my disciple." (Luke 14:26)

In conclusion, I feel there is a clear lesson for us in this Gospel passage; we are being challenged to examine our attitudes, our priorities, our relationships with one another and, most importantly, our relationship with God.

That *narrow gate* means we MUST have a **GOD FIRST** approach to everything we do.

28

My Different Thoughts

This reflection will look at the Parable about the owner of a vineyard and his way of paying his laborers.

While I am sure you are familiar with the story, I feel I should paraphrase it before I offer my thoughts.

Jesus told his disciples this Parable:

> *Jesus compared the kingdom of heaven to a landowner who hired laborers to work in his vineyard. He hired the first group at nine o'clock; he then hired a second group around noon and, again, a group at three o'clock and a final group at five o'clock. When it came time to pay them, he gave the same wages to those who started at five as those who started at nine. Needless to say, the group who began at nine were not happy, feeling that was unfair. The landowner explained EACH had hired on at the usual daily wage,*

so they received what they were owed. It matters not, if he generously gave the same wage to those who worked fewer hours. (Matthew 20:1–20)

First, I will point out that this parable is found ONLY in Matthew's Gospel.

As a reminder, a parable, by scriptural definition, is a simple story told by Jesus in his teaching to illustrate a moral or spiritual lesson.

There are several ways a person could interpret this parable. One I read suggested that Jesus was trying to advise the Jews in the crowd that they should not assume that just because they were the first called by God that they would receive a greater reward for their acceptance than others; likely, referring to the Gentiles who came to believe later.

I disagree with that interpretation because of the beginning sentence: "Jesus told his DISCIPLES this parable." In as much as Jesus used *The Parable* as a teaching tool, what was he trying to *teach his disciples*? Before addressing that question, I want to point to this prior passage: Then Peter addressed him saying, 'Behold, we have left all and followed thee; what then shall we have"? To which Jesus responded, "And everyone who has left house, or brothers, or sisters, or father, or mother, or wife or children, or hands, for my name's sake shall receive a hundredfold and shall possess life everlasting. **But many who are first NOW will be last and many who are last now will be first."** (Matthew 19:27–30)

Then, Jesus went on to tell them the parable of the landowner/vineyard. I just do not think his teaching had anything to do with fairness or justice. It seems to me that Peter, with his question, was referring to a "pecking order" in heaven; and I believe Jesus was trying to change the mind of Peter, and that of all the apostles, from "a place mentality" to a broader view of God's love of all people who strive daily to do the will of the Father and to live their lives in accord with Jesus' Gospel message. Their love of God and God's love for them, then, is the picture of *heaven*.

AND there are no chairs!

29

The Ten Lepers

Our passage for study today is the familiar story of Jesus' encounter with ten lepers. This passage is from the Gospel of Luke; it is described only in his Gospel which is interesting to me and unclear as to why.

In our reading, we find that Jesus was passing between Galilee and Samaria while making his way from Nazareth to Jerusalem; upon entering a village ten lepers met him. Tradition has it that nine were Jews and one was a Samaritan. The disease had, obviously, done away with the centuries old political and religious disagreements between the two groups; but that is a topic for another day.

I have dealt with the disease in a prior reflection and after I read this passage, I decided to do some research. At the risk of providing more on the subject than one needs or desires to know, I will share the results of my effort. I found the best information on the subject in the Book of Leviticus from the Old Testament;

there, I found, outlined, the duties performed by the Offices and Ministries for Priests and Levites. In addition, in Chapter 13:45–46, I read: "and a leper in whom the plague is, his clothes shall he rent, and his head bared, and he shall put a covering upon his lip." Further, Leviticus outlines the full set of laws and proscribed practices for the disease of leprosy which had been handed down by God to Moses and Aaron: "the man in whose skin or flesh shall arise a different color, a blister or as it were something shining, that is the stroke of leprosy. Such a man, having discovered what looks like leprosy in his skin must go and show himself to a priest, who would, after performing the required rites, decide his fate. If the priest declared the man to have leprosy, he would pronounce him ceremoniously unclean. Thereafter, the afflicted person had to live outside the community with no interpersonal association and when about to come near anyone, other than a fellow leper, be required to cry out, **unclean**, **unclean** to prevent any physical contact". Simply put, a leper was a complete social outcast.

With that information, we return to our Gospel passage:

There met him ten men that were lepers who stood afar off, and they lifted up their voice crying:

*"Jesus, **Master**, have mercy on us." When he saw them, he said to them: "go show yourselves to the priests." AND IT CAME TO PASS THAT AS THEY WENT, THEY WERE MADE CLEAN!*

But one of them, when he saw that he was healed, turned back and WITH A LOUD VOICE GLORIFYING GOD and he fell on his face at His feet, giving thanks; and he was a Samaritan.

But Jesus answered and said: "Were not the ten made clean? But where are the nine? Has no one been found

> *to return and give glory to God except this foreigner"?*
> *And he said to him: "Arise, go thy way, for thy faith has*
> *SAVED THEE." (Luke 17:11–19)*

Now, let us take a closer look; I believe the main points can be found in several key words:

> **Master**—This indicates they knew about Jesus, his teachings and implied authority.
>
> **Faith**—Their cry for mercy tells us they were men of *faith* who believed Jesus could help them.
>
> **Obedience**—In order for their faith to be rewarded they had to obey Jesus' command.
>
> **Trust**—They trusted Jesus and went away to a priest without question or delay.

And when he saw them, and heard their cry he responded to their prayer:

> **Compassion**—Jesus recognized them as lepers, outcasts, the lowest of the low. "The Lord is near to all who call upon him. To all who call upon him in truth." (Psalm 145:18)
>
> **Omnipotent**—Without ever getting close to them, Jesus healed them from "afar" with but his **Word**.
>
> **Spiritual Healing**—Jesus said: "Arise, go thy way thy faith has SAVED thee." "Our Lord truly has a greater desire to give than we do to receive; and he has a greater desire to show us mercy than we do to see ourselves freed of our wretchedness." St Augustine

And Jesus said: "Were not the ten made clean? But where are the nine?"

> **Gratitude**—Jesus noted the lack of gratitude by the other nine.

In this story, we see that God's love extends to everyone. Since, in the Bible, disease equates to sinfulness, Jesus offers his healing grace to ALL SINNERS who come to him in faith.

Everyone, in faith, is invited to approach Jesus with their disease (sins) and **trust** in his mercy.

Each of us have been blessed; but do we take the time to acknowledge that everything we have is a gift from God? When our prayers are answered, do we first enjoy His grace (blessing) like the nine or do we first give **thanks** to God like the lowly Samaritan? I conclude with this thought: **GOD NOTICES!**

"Were not the ten made clean? But where are the nine?"

30

The Great Delay

This reflection will examine the miracle of Jesus raising Lazarus from the dead, the last of Jesus' miracles according to John. It is also, for me, a challenge.

Interestingly, the story is described *only* in John's Gospel. When such an event is not included in any of the Synoptic Gospels it always makes me wonder. However, in this instance, there seems to be a plausible explanation which I will explain later.

Since our passage is quite lengthy, I will paraphrase it, and, hopefully, not leave out salient facts:

Followers and friends of Jesus, Mary, and her sister Martha, had a brother named Lazarus who became seriously ill, so they sent word to Jesus. When Jesus heard he said: "This sickness is not unto death *but for the glory of God* that through it the Son of God may be glorified." After getting the news, Jesus remained where he was for two more days. Then he said to his disciples: "Lazarus, our friend, sleeps. But I go that I may wake him from sleep." Later, when his disciples did not understand, he said to them plainly: "Lazarus is dead, and I rejoice on your account that I was not there **that you may believe**." Jesus therefore came and found Martha and Mary in mourning. Hearing Jesus was coming, Martha went to meet him, saying: "Lord, if you had been here my brother would not have died." Jesus replied: "Thy brother shall **rise**." By that time, Lazarus had been in the tomb **four days**. Regardless, he asked that the stone covering the tomb be rolled back and then he said: "Lazarus come forth." *And at once, he who had been dead came forth bound feet and hands with bandages, and his face was tied up with a cloth.* (John 11:1–44)

Earlier I remarked that this, for me, is a challenging story on several levels. For instance, Jesus, obviously, knew Lazarus was ill BEFORE word was sent to him. Still, he made no effort to prevent his death; in fact, he stayed where he was for two more days. Consequently, he **willingly allowed** the pain and sorrow of Lazarus' sisters and those around them. Why? Even more perplexing, how could Lazarus come out of the tomb with his feet and hands bound with bandages?

As I have stated in previous reflections, certain words have special meaning; Here, I point to a word found often in our passage—**BELIEVE**. Jesus said to them (disciples): "Lazarus is dead; and I rejoice on your account that I was not there that you may **believe**." Later, Jesus said to her (Martha): "thy brother shall **rise**." And "I am the **RESURRECTION** and the life; he who **believes** in me, even if he dies shall live; and whoever lives and **believes** in me shall never die. Do you **believe** this"? "Yes, Lord I **believe**;" she replied.

Before I offer my thoughts on the meaning of this passage, it is worth noting that the event took place near the end of Jesus' earthly ministry and Jesus was having difficulty getting the apostles to understand his teaching. i.e., "Though you have eyes to see do you still not see." (Mark 8:18).

Therefore, I conclude this miracle was PLANNED by Jesus for two purposes: First, he needed a powerful event to get through to the apostles, as well as teach his followers that ALL things were possible **if they believed in the power of God**. Second, with the *resurrecting* of Lazarus he wanted to *foreshadow* his own death and resurrection, knowing that in doing so he would inspire the people following him, which it did with a triumphant entry into Jerusalem, as well as provoke the hatred of the Jewish religious leaders and motivate them to want to get rid of him, which they did on Good Friday.

To me, an interesting back story, and a lesson for us, is that in delaying his journey for two days, Jesus allowed his good friends Martha and Mary to suffer their brother's illness and death. Isn't that true in our own lives as well? Don't we sometimes feel God is not listening when our prayers go unanswered for a longer period than we would like?

Now, back to the question as to why none of the Synoptic Gospel authors included this miracle in their gospels. The prevailing theory is that when they wrote their Gospels in mid first century Lazarus was still living and their including the event would likely have motivated the Jewish religious leaders to kill him also; whereas John did not write his Gospel until near the end of the first century and times had changed significantly, by then.

31

Taking a Closer Look

Occasionally, after reading a passage in Scripture, I realize a "once through" left me wondering if there might be more meaning to be gleaned. Such was the case with Luke 18:15–17.

Before we take that *closer look*, we will do a little review; it is noteworthy that by this time Jesus was well into his journey to Jerusalem. And we should also note that the disciples referenced in the passage had been with him for some time. Here we are in Chapter 18; the story of the selection of the 12 took place way back in Chapter 6. Thus, they had seen and heard a lot, but did they *understand*? Let's take a look:

Now they were bringing the babes also to him that he might touch them; but when the disciples saw it, they rebuked them. But Jesus called them together and said, "Let the little children come to me, and do not hinder them, for of such is the kingdom of God. Amen I say to you, whoever does not accept the kingdom of God as a little child will not enter into it."

Of interest, this scenario is played out in all three Synoptic Gospels, in addition, I would point out what I found interesting and unusual: The words *for of such is the kingdom of God* are identical in all three. That indicates to me those are the **key words** in the passage.

Before we get to that, let's look at another aspect: "And they were bringing the babes to him that he might touch them; **but when the disciples saw it, they rebuked them**; but when he saw them, he called them together and ordered: **"Let the little children come to me."** (In Matthew's Gospel Jesus didn't just call them together, *he was indignant*.) Why? Because shortly before that we find this passage: Now a discussion arose among them as to which of them was the greatest. But Jesus knowing the reasoning of their heart, took a **little child** and set him at his side and said to them: Whoever receives this **little child** for my sake receives me." (Luke 9:46–48)

So yes, Jesus was frustrated with the disciple's lack of understanding of his love for little children as well as their still not showing they had a grasp on the nature of the kingdom of God as it pertains to the widowed and children; those unable to fend for themselves.

Now, let's get back to those **key words**: "for of such is the kingdom of God." I use the word "key" because they were not intended for just the disciples; they were intended for the crowd that had followed him and YES for you and me. Typically, *key words* are teaching words.

What is the kingdom of God? There are many detailed, educated answers; but to me it can be summed up in one word—**GRACE** which would entail the essence of God's very nature—LOVE. In that sense, the kingdom of God would be the state of enjoying the unmerited favor of God's love.

Now then, how do we get there? Jesus tells us plainly; we must become like a child; but what does that mean? A child has an open mind, willing to listen and learn and be, generally, willing to accept that which is being taught. A child has an open heart, accepting the love that is offered without questioning. A child trusts implicitly. These are huge hurdles for most of us. So where do we start—**PRAYER**. We can all pray! There is no right or wrong way to do that. No special time or place; after all, God sees us coming. He already knows what is in our heart. No particular religion or belief is required—just a willingness to talk to God.

Let's hope the disciples learned from their experience in this story. And let's hope we too can learn from our having reflected on this passage.

32

My Man—Bartimeus

As I have mentioned previously, Jesus worked 37 miracles during his time on Earth including eight where he gave sight to a blind person. Of all those stories in Scripture, this one about the blind Bartimeus is my favorite. Hopefully, by the time you reach the end of this reflection, you will understand why.

Although the event is described in all three Synoptic Gospels, albeit with some minor differences, I chose to follow Mark's version; and I feel it best to include the entire passage:

> And they came to Jericho. And, as he was leaving Jericho with his disciples and a very large crowd, Bartimeus, a blind man, the son of Timeus, was sitting by the wayside, begging. And hearing that it was Jesus of Nazareth, he began to cry out and say, "Jesus, Son of David, have mercy on me!" And many angrily tried to silence him. But he cried out all the louder, "Son of David, have mercy on me!" Then Jesus

> *stopped and commanded that he should be called. And they called the blind man and said to him, "Take courage. Get up, he is calling thee." And throwing off his cloak, he sprang to his feet and came to him. And Jesus addressed him, saying, "What wouldst thou have me do for thee?" And the blind man said to him, "Rabboni, that I may see." And Jesus said to him, "Go thy way thy faith has saved thee." And at once he received his sight and followed him along the road.* (Mark 10:46–52)

It should be noted that this miracle took place late during Jesus' earthly ministry. In fact, he was preparing for his FINAL entry into Jerusalem where he would be crucified. As indicated, he was accompanied by a very large crowd; I am envisioning a chaotic scene.

As a reminder, in that culture, any affliction, physical, mental or emotional was felt to have resulted from a sin committed by the person so afflicted or by his or her parents.

Further, my research showed that at that time and in that part of the world, diseases of the eye were common; blindness/begging was commonplace; Bartimeus was just one of many.

Let us review the highlights of the event:

- As he was sitting by the wayside begging and hearing it was Jesus of Nazareth, he began to cry out," Jesus, Son of David, have mercy on me."

- Bartimeus was a beggar, but he knew a lot about Jesus and what he had done.

- Bartimeus REACHED out to Jesus in prayer: "Jesus, have

mercy on me."

- Bartimeus PERSISTED, even though the crowd tried to silence him.

- Bartimeus was a FOLLOWER of Jesus addressing him as "Rabboni."

- Bartimeus **threw off his cloak** and sprang to his feet. He TRUSTED that he would get a new way of life; WHAT GREAT FAITH in the mercy of Jesus!

- "Go thy way, thy **faith** has saved thee!" At once he received his sight and **followed him along the road**. Bartimeus was healed PHYSICALLY and SPIRITUALLY.

Why did Bartimeus impress me so?

- He accepted God's will for his fate in life but remained FAITHFUL, accepting his CROSS.
- He did not hesitate to cry out to Jesus in prayer.
- Upon receiving his sight, Bartimeus did not go off to enjoy his new way of life; rather **he followed him along the road**.

Question to consider:

WHAT DOES IT MEAN TO FOLLOW JESUS ALONG THE ROAD?

33

Are You Just a Fig Leaf?

I have written previously: Wherefore you shall stumble, there shall you dig.

Well, I stumbled upon Mark 11:11–26; and ended up finding the story worth a "dig." Since it is a lengthy passage, I will paraphrase it and hope I don't miss any salient points.

As always, I believe it will be helpful to understand the story to set the scene. At the beginning of Chapter 11, Mark describes Jesus' triumphant entry into Jerusalem riding on a colt and with an adoring crowd littering the road in front of him with their cloaks and with tree branches. Upon his arrival in Jerusalem, he went **into the temple area and looked around at everything** and, since it was late in the day, he went out to the village of Bethany with his apostles.

Then our passage picks up the following morning; Jesus was hungry and seeing a **LEAFY** fig tree he approached but found no figs as it was too early in the season. But he then spoke: "May no one ever eat fruit of thee henceforward forever." Coming again into Jerusalem and entering the temple, he became angry, casting out the sellers and buyers of pigeons and doves which were being made available for *sacrifice* according to Jewish religious rites; he overturned the tables of the moneychangers saying: "Is it not written, my house shall be called a house of prayer for all the nations; but you have made it a den of thieves." Following that episode, he spent the day there teaching, and upon leaving, they again passed by the fig tree which they found to be **withered**.

So, what are we to make of this? I would submit that Jesus knew there would be no figs on that tree; and I believe that in reading the passage, we need to tie the two parts together: the withered fig tree and Jesus' "tantrum" with the marketing activities in the temple. Hopefully, I can support those assertions.

My research turned up this in Luke's Gospel, Chapter 13:6–9; Jesus, earlier, offered the "Parable of the Fig Tree" in his teaching: There a man had a fig tree planted and upon finding it did not produce fruit ordered it cut down. Interestingly, however, Luke did not describe a "withered" fig tree in his Gospel. Now curious, I turned to Matthew' Gospel and I found that he did include a "withered" fig tree, BUT there is, among the authors, a significant variance in detail; whereas Mark has Peter noticing the withered fig tree the **next day after** the incident in the temple, Matthew has Peter seeing the withered tree **the same day** that Jesus condemned it. (Matthew 21:18) Does it matter? I think so. Mark **separates** the withered tree and temple dustup by a day; whereas by having the tree wither immediately after the curse is pronounced, Matthew **drives the narrative forward** to Jesus clearing the temple.

Again, I believe, that since Jesus knew there would be no figs at that time of the year, he used the **withered** tree as a metaphor;

the fig tree being an obvious reference to the Jew's spiritual sterility. Recall, previously, Jesus had used the Parable of the Fig Tree to teach about the woes of unproductive faith. Accordingly, that imagery would fit here and would, perhaps, remind his Jewish listeners of the words of the Prophet Isaiah from the Old Testament: "The vineyard of the Lord of hosts is the house of Israel, and the men of Judah are his pleasant planting; and he looked for justice, but behold, bloodshed; for righteousness, but behold a cry." (Isaiah 5:7)

I conclude, therefore, that the theme of our passage is the spiritual "fruitlessness" of the Jewish people who through their "sacrificial rites," gave the *appearance* of spiritual production, but as the prophet foretold, alas, none.

Whereas it might be easy to view this story as simply a judgment on Israel's *spiritual state*, we should not overlook the practical application it holds for us, as well. Although by regular church attendance we may give the **appearance** of being spiritually productive, the question remains, what did we do in our daily lives, thereafter, to spread the message of Jesus in the world? Are we a "leafy" **fruitful** community? Or would Jesus find us to be a "withered non-productive" Christian community?

Going forward, as we strive to be **fruitful Christians**, we would do well to heed these words from Jesus at the Last Supper: "He who abides in me, and I in him, he it is that bears much fruit." (John 15:5)

34

The Marriage Feast

As I have indicated in previous reflections, Jesus frequently used the parable in his teaching; in fact, he used it between 30 and 50 times depending on which source you accept. We will study one of those parables in this reflection; in doing so we will examine the Gospels of both Matthew and Luke; they both described the event, albeit with differences, where Jesus compared the kingdom of heaven to a wedding banquet.

As usual, I think it is helpful to include a bit of background information; we saw in Chapter 21 of Matthew the Parable of the Vinedressers in which Jesus took aim at the Jewish chief priests and Pharisees. That Chapter ended with these words: And when the chief priests and Pharisees had heard his parables, they knew that he was speaking about them. And though they sought to lay hands on him, they feared the people, because they regarded him as a prophet.

With that information, we now read Matthew's version of our passage:

> And Jesus addressed them (chief priests and Pharisees) and spoke to them again in parables, saying: "The kingdom of heaven is like a king who made a marriage feast for his son. And he sent his servants to call in those invited to the marriage feast; but they would not come. Again, he sent out other servants, saying, tell those who are invited, behold I have prepared my dinner; my oxen and fatlings are killed, and everything is ready; come to the marriage feast; but they made light of it, and went off, one to his farm, and another to his business; and the rest laid hold of his servants, treated them shamefully, and killed them.
>
> But, when the king heard of it, he was angry; and he sent his armies, who destroyed those murderers, and burnt their city; then he said to his servants, the marriage feast indeed is ready; but those who were invited were not worthy; go therefore to the crossroads, and invite to the marriage feast whomever you shall find. And his servants went out into the roads and gathered all who they found both good and bad; and the marriage feast was filled with guests.
>
> Now the king went in to see the guests and he saw there a man who had not on a wedding garment. And he said to him, "friend, how didst thou come in here without a wedding garment?" But he was speechless. Then the king said to the attendants, "bind his hands and feet and cast him forth into the darkness outside where there will be weeping and the gnash-

ing of teeth; for many are called but few are chosen." (Matthew 22:1–14)

To examine the differences between Matthew's and Luke's Gospels, we need to read Luke's description of the event:

> But he said to them, "a certain man gave a great supper, and he invited many. And he sent his servant at supper time to tell those invited to come for everything is now ready. And they all with one accord began to excuse themselves. The first said to him, "I have bought a farm, and I must go out and see it; I pray thee hold me excused." And another said, "I have bought five yoke of oxen, and I am on my way to try them. I pray thee hold me excused." And another said, "I have married a wife and therefore I can't come". And the servant returned and reported these things to his master. Then the master of the house was angry and said to the servant" Go out quickly into the streets and lanes of the city and bring in here the poor and the crippled and the blind and the lame". And the servant said, "Sir, thy order has been carried out and still there is room". Then the master said to the servant "Go out into the highways and hedges and make them come in so that my house may be filled. For I tell you that none of those who were invited shall taste of my supper." (Luke 14:16–24)

These are two quite different versions of the same event but with the same message: A king (God the Father) sent His son (Jesus) to marry His people (Israel) and in accordance with Jewish culture planned a wedding banquet (heaven); He invited his constituents (Jewish people), but they refused His invitation. In anger, He took away their preferred status and opened His banquet (His promise of salvation) to All, which includes us if we wear His wedding garment (His holy Word).

Matthew's Jewish community for whom he penned his Gospel, being knowledgeable about the Old Testament, could relate to a wedding banquet, the killing of the servants as well as the significance of the wedding garment. According to their custom, all guests were REQUIRED to wear the garment which was supplied by the banquet host. Certainly, the self-righteous Pharisees, who heard this parable, did not miss Jesus' point; for in the very next verse we read, "the Pharisees went out and laid plans to trap him in his words."

The message in the parable is clear: God punished the Jewish people not because they **did not** accept His invitation to the Wedding Feast but because they **chose not to** accept.

Finally, what stands out to me is the first line in Matthew's description: "And Jesus addressed them (Pharisees) and spoke to them in **parables**." I think, as noted, in his description of this encounter, Matthew alluded to the Old Testament, which he often did in his Gospel, with the "killing of the king's servants" and the "binding hand and foot" of the guest without a wedding garment.

But in either or both descriptions of the event studied, Jesus' message is that God's invitation is extended to anyone who will set aside his own *righteousness* and, by faith, accept the gift of the righteousness which God offered through Christ. Indeed, our wedding garment IS the righteousness of Christ and unless we have that we will miss the heavenly feast. As Matthew made clear, we **must respond positively** to that gift (invitation). ALAS, those invited to the King's Wedding Dinner did not and they paid a heavy price!

FOR MANY ARE CALLED, BUT FEW ARE CHOSEN!

35

Judas the Iscariot–Why?

We are entering Holy Week, an important time in the liturgical year. Soon we will be at Good Friday and focusing on the crucifixion of Jesus.

Why then, you may well be wondering, am I doing a reflection on the apostle, Judas the Iscariot. The fact is that there is something about his being an apostle that has always intrigued me. At first, I thought it might be his name; "*Iscariot*" just sounds evil, so I did some research and found that "Iscariot" is just a town in Judea.

Jesus chooses the apostles:

> *And when the day broke, he summoned his* **disciples**; *and from these he chose twelve (whom he also named apostles) (Luke 6:13–14)*

Interestingly, Scripture shows that a sizable number of the apostles were from Galilee. Moreover, several were fishermen at the Sea of Galilee; and Matthew, who as we know, was a tax collector. ONLY Judas the Iscariot was an outsider being from the tribe of Judah.

From the beginning, Judas was not popular with the other apostles:

> *Then one of the apostles, Judas Iscariot, he who was about to betray him, said, "Why was this ointment not sold for three hundred denary, and given to the poor?" Now he said this not because he cared for the poor but because he was a thief, and holding the purse, used to take out what was put in it. (John 12:4–7)*

And even Jesus did not seem to care for him:

> *Therefore, Jesus said to Judas, "**Let her be**, that she may keep it for the day of my burial. For the poor you have always with you, but you do not always have me." (John 12:7–8)*

Moreover, Jesus seemed to be well aware Judas was a betrayer:

> *Jesus answered them, "Have I not chosen you, the Twelve? Yet, one of you is a devil." (John 6:71–72)*

One has to wonder, then, why then did Jesus **choose** Judas the Iscariot? Let's start by reading another passage: Jesus said, "while I was with them, I kept them in thy name. Those whom thou hast given me I guarded and not one of them perished except the **son of perdition in order that the SCRIPTURE BE FULFILLED**." What Scripture was Jesus referring to? Note this, also, Jesus said, "even so, must the Son of Man be lifted up that those who believe in hm may not perish, but may have life everlasting. For God did not **SEND HIS SON** into the world to judge the world but that the world *might be saved through him.*" (John 3:17)

Items of note:

- God **sent** His Son, Jesus into the world for the salvation of all men.

- Jesus was betrayed by one of those **chosen** to be an apostle.

- Jesus did not like Judas.

- Jesus gave his life in expiation of sins of ALL people.

All the above show God's **MASTER PLAN** and reflects His love and mercy. Jesus had a role to play, representing a **New Covenant** for the salvation of all mankind. Judas also played a role representing the Jewish people who **betrayed** their Covenant with God as reflected in the Old Testament.

Now the question: WHY DID HE CHOOSE JUDAS?

My thought:

Jesus DID NOT choose Judas; he "appointed" him. Judas was **CHOSEN** by the Father! Jesus accepted Judas in order that God's **plan of salvation** might be fulfilled.

THY WILL BE DONE!

36

What Does it Mean to be Prepared?

We previously studied several parables mostly from Chapter 13 of Matthew's Gospel. Those were just a few of the more than 30 parables utilized by Jesus during his time of instructing his followers about the kingdom of heaven. Our study has continued to the point where we find him **preparing** his followers, and us, for when his time on Earth is finished; and he did so in the context of the "end time" or "judgement day." The time of Crucifixion was rapidly approaching!

For this reflection, we will study the parable known as the Parable of the Ten Virgins found in Chapter 25 of Matthew's Gospel. However, before we get there, we need to spend a little time on Chapter 24; there, we read that Jesus was exhorting his disciples, "Watch therefore, for you do not know at what hour your Lord is to come; but be assured, that if the householder had known at what hour the thief was coming, he would have watched and not have let his house be broken into. *Therefore, you MUST be ready because at an hour that you do not expect, the Son of Man WILL COME."*

With that sobering thought we proceed to Chapter 25:

Parable of the Ten Virgins

> *Then will the kingdom of heaven be like ten virgins who took their lamps and went forth to meet the bridegroom and the bride. Five of them were foolish and five wise; but the five foolish, when taking their lamps took no oil in their vessels while the wise did take oil in their vessels. Then as the bridegroom was long in coming, they became drowsy and slept, and at midnight a cry arose: "Behold, the bridegroom is coming, go forth to meet him." Then, all those virgins arose and trimmed their lamps. And the foolish said to the wise, "Give us some of your oil, for our lamps are going out." The wise answered saying, "Lest there may not be enough for us and for you, go rather to those who sell it and buy some for yourselves."*
>
> *Now while they were gone to buy it, the bridegroom came; and those who were ready went in with him to the marriage feast, and the door was shut. Finally, there also came the other virgins who said, "Sir, sir, open the door for us!" But he answered and said, "Amen I say to you I do not know you." Watch therefore, for you know neither the day nor the hour.* (Matthew 25:1–13)

Clearly, from Chapter 24 through the Parable of the Ten Virgins, Jesus makes CLEAR the necessity to always be **prepared** for the end of OUR time on earth. Therein lies the simple but powerful message of this parable.

Now just a quick look at our chosen passage as described by Matthew. We have a **bridegroom** (Jesus). We are told there were ten virgins (bridesmaids)—five wise and five foolish. The story is about **PREPARATION** and five were declared "foolish" because they did not bring enough oil for their lamps.

I do not agree that they were **FOOLISH**. Let's look at the facts:

- The FIVE "foolish" were virgins = bridesmaids.
- They arrived on time with their lamps full of oil.
- They waited with the "wise" five.
- They fell asleep same as the "wise."
- When alerted they trimmed their lamps same as the "wise".
- The bridegroom was late!

The "wise virgins" refused to share their ABUNDANCE of oil. The "foolish" virgins had no choice but to leave and purchase more oil. While they were gone, the bridegroom (Jesus) arrived, and the door was shut. Upon their return they pleaded to be let in, but he answered and said, "Amen, I say to you, I do not know you."

Does that sound like Jesus? So, what is going on?

I submit the culprit is Matthew. His Gospel was penned for recent Jewish converts. Thus, he was writing for a Jewish community. Moreover, his Gospel contains numerous references to the Old Testament where, as we know, God delivered strict and harsh judgements. Finally, recall that in the prevailing culture of

Matthew's time, women were not held in high esteem, and you can see where I'm coming from. They were adequately prepared BUT FOR THE BRIDEGROOM'S DELAY IN ARRIVING!

I agree that they were not **PREPARED**; but **THEY WERE NOT FOOLISH**!

37

Walking the Final Mile With Jesus

In previous reflections we have studied the WORDS and WORKS of Jesus from the Jordan to Jerusalem where his earthly ministry ended in death, all as he dutifully **carried out the will of his Father**.

The reflections are gleaned from the writings of all four Gospel authors, including three occasions where the *voice of the Father was heard*, the last of which we cover in this effort.

I have tried to be judicious with referencing passages from the Old Testament; however, I feel these words from the Prophet Isaiah relate to what will turn out to be the final paragraph of this reflection:

> *But he was wounded for our iniquities; he was bruised for our sins. And the Lord was pleased to bruise him in infirmity, if he shall lay down his life for sin, and he shall see a long-lived seed; and the will of the Lord shall be prosperous in his hand. (Isaiah 53:5–10)*

Clearly, Jesus knew his role in the Father's desire/plan that all persons should have the opportunity to be saved from their sins and have eternal life.

We begin our walk:

> *Jesus therefore said to them, "When you have lifted up the Son of Man then will you know that I am he." (John 8:23)*
>
> *"Abraham, your father, rejoiced that he was to see my day. He saw it and was glad." The Jews therefore said to him, "Thou are not yet fifty years old and hast thou seen Abraham?" Jesus said to them, "Amen, amen, I say to you before Abraham came to be, I am." They therefore **took up stones to cast at him**, but Jesus hid himself and went out of the temple. (John 8:58–59)*
>
> *And as he was passing by, he saw a man blind from birth. And his disciples asked him, "Rabbi, who has sinned the man or his parents that he should be born blind?" Jesus answered, "Neither has this man sinned nor his parents, **but** the works of God were to be manifest in him. I must do the works of him who sent me while it is still day; night is coming when no one can work. **As long as I am in the world, I am the light of the world.** For judgment have I come into this world, that they who **do not see may see** and they who see may become blind." And some of the Pharisees who were with him heard this and they said to him, "are we blind?" Jesus said to them, "if you were blind you would not have sin. But now that you say, 'we see' **your sin remains**." (John 9:39–41)*

Again, there arose a division among the Jews; many were saying, "he has a devil and is mad." Others were saying, "These are not the words of one who has a devil. Can a devil open the eyes of the blind?" (John 10:21)

Jesus answered them, "What my Father has given me is greater than all. And no one is able to snatch anything out of the hand of my Father. **I and the Father are one.***" The Jews therefore took up stones to stone him. Jesus answered them, "Many good works have I shown you from my Father. For which of these do you stone me?" The Jews answered him, "Not for a good work do we stone you but for* **blasphemy, and because thou, being a man, makest thyself God.***" Jesus said, "If I do not perform the works of my Father, do not believe me. But if I do perform them and you're not willing to believe me, believe the works, that you may know and believe that* **the Father is in me and I in the Father***." THEY SOUGHT TO SEIZE HIM; and he went forth out of their hands. (John 10:29–39)*

And Jesus, raising his eyes, said, "Father, I give thee **thanks** *that thou hast heard me. Yet, I knew that thou always hearest me; but because of the people who stand around I spoke; that they may believe that* **thou hast sent me.***" When he had said this, he cried out with a loud voice:* **"LAZARUS, come forth."** *And at once he who had been dead came forth, bound feet and hands, and his face was tied up with a cloth. Jesus said to them, "Unbind him and let him go." Many therefore of the Jews who had come to Mary, and had seen what he did, believed in him. But some of them went away to the Pharisees and told them the things* *that Jesus had done. The chief priests and the Pharisees therefore gathered together a council and said, "What are we doing? For this man is working many signs.* **If we let him alone as he is, all will believe in him, and the Romans will come AND TAKE AWAY OUR PLACE AND OUR NATION.***" (John 11:48)*

****FROM THAT DAY FORTH THEIR PLAN WAS TO PUT HIM TO DEATH****

And certain Gentiles had gone up to worship and said to Phillip, "Sir we wish to see Jesus." Phillip spoke to Jesus, But Jesus answered them:

"The hour has come for the Son of Man to be glorified"

Now my soul is troubled. And what shall I say? "Father, save me from this hour?" No, this is why I came to this hour: "Father, **glorify thy name***!" And there came therefore A VOICE FROM HEAVEN:* **"I have both glorified it and I will glorify it again."** *Jesus said: "Not for me did this voice come* **but for you***. Now is the judgment of the world; now will the prince of the world be cast out.* **And I, if I be lifted up from the earth, will draw all things to myself.***" (John 12:23–32)*

Now the Passover was drawing near; and the chief priests and the Scribes were seeking how they might put him to death. But Satan entered into Judas, and he went away and discussed how he might betray him to them. (Luke 22:3–4)

Jesus desired to eat the Passover meal with his disciples: Jesus said, "but behold the hand of him who betrays me is with me on the table. For the Son of Man indeed goes his way as it HAS BEEN DETERMINED." (Luke 22:21–23)

*And they came to Gethsemane, and he said, "Sit down while **I pray**." And he fell on his face and said, **"Abba, Father, all things are possible with thee. REMOVE THIS CUP FROM ME; yet not what I Will but thou WILLEST."** (Mark 14:32–36)*

*And while he was yet speaking, Judas Iscariot came and with him a great crowd with swords and clubs from the chief priests and the Scribes and the elders; and they **seized him and held him**. (Matthew 26:47)*

*Pilate said to the crowd, "What then do you want me to do with the king of the Jews?" But they cried out, **"CRUCIFY HIM."** They mocked him, placed a crown of thorns on his head and brought him to a place called Golgotha. (Luke 23:18)*

THEY CRUCIFIED HIM!

*It was about the sixth hour, and there was darkness over the whole land and Jesus cried out: **"Father, into thy hands I commend my spirit."** Having said that he expired. (Luke 24:44–46)*

Lord, have mercy! Christ, have mercy!

38

The Letter to the Romans

Although I struggle with Paul's style of writing as found in his Letters among the books in the New Testament and not always in complete agreement with his views, in order that my effort here be thorough, I decided I needed to do a reflection on one of his Letters. I settled on his Letter to the Romans which appears first among his Letters in my Bible, although, it was not the first of his Letters.

The Letter to the Romans was written while he was in Corinth in 57-58 A.D. and planning to visit Rome while on his way to Spain. That Letter followed numerous other letters he penned to churches he had established, mostly in Asia Minor. But, in advance of his visit to Rome, he chose to address, more fully, the question of the period having to do with the "way to heaven." Accordingly, he penned to the Romans his expanded view of justification by faith, while noting how that might relate to the law of Moses under which the Jews had lived for centuries.

At its core, the book of Romans is about **FAITH** in Jesus Christ and Paul set forth, strongly, "we have been *justified by faith*."

Through 16 pages Paul asserts:

- Everyone has sinned and is in need of **Salvation**.

- **Salvation** is a *gift* made available to us through *FAITH* in Christ

- *FAITH* and acceptance of God's grace are sufficient for **Salvation**.

- Human efforts (good works) can <u>never</u> *earn* **Salvation**.

Later, around 62–63 A.D., James, the Apostle, wrote his own Letter/Epistle, wherein he exhorts Jewish Christians by setting forth his ideas for practical Christian living. Of note were his views on faith and works:

> *What will it profit, my brethren, if a man says he has faith but does not have works? Can faith save him? And if a brother or sister be naked and in want of daily food, and one of you say to them, "Go in Peace, be warmed and filled," yet you do not give them what is necessary for the body, what does it profit? So,* **faith too, unless it has works is dead in itself.** *But if someone will say, "Thou hast faith, and I have works." Show me thy faith without works, and I from my works will show thee my faith.* … **Faith without works is useless.**

Also of interest, Paul had touched on the issue of faith and works in his letter to the Galatians. Written in 54 A.D. and while addressing Cephas (Peter): "We are Jews by birth and not sinners from among the Gentiles. But we know that man is not justified by the **works of the law** but by the **faith of Jesus Christ**. Hence, we also believe in Christ Jesus that we may be **justified** by the **FAITH of Christ** and not by the **Works** of the **LAW**; because by the **Works** of the **LAW** no man will be **JUSTIFIED**."

Little did he realize the question of the relationship between faith and works to salvation would continue to be debated, even to the present time.

However, that debate was sharpened when Martin Luther, at the time of the Reformation, cited Romans in his writings in what, later, evolved into the Lutheran Religion. Luther seized upon 3:21: "But now the justice of God has been made manifest independently of the Law." Then 3:28: "For we reckon that a man is justified by faith independently of the works of the law." Luther then added the word "alone" in his writing, which came to be known as the doctrine of "Sola Fide"—faith alone. The ongoing debate between Religions is centered on the word—justification, which is a legal term signifying acquittal.

As I have done previously, I believe it is important to add perspective by looking at the *scene*. Paul was continuing to preach the Word to the Gentiles, hoping to bring them into the Church. However, some Jewish authorities, including Peter (see previous comment) argued that the Gentiles should comply with all the requirements of the Mosaic law, which would include circumcision. There were over six hundred separate commandments in that "law, a violation of any one of them would render a person *unjust*.

Somewhere along the way, due mainly to the Reformation, Works of the Law was filtered and in later discussion the argument became that **works** of any kind are not only unnecessary but of no importance at all as they relate to *justification*. See Sola fide.

I humbly proffer that was not what Paul was saying, especially in Galatians; there he preached that one cannot be saved by **works of the law**, obviously wishing to distinguish the Mosaic law from the tenets of Jesus' teaching based on love of God and love of neighbor. There, the key to salvation is faith in Jesus Christ and his promise of salvation if we love God, love our neighbor, and obey his commandments. My question then is HOW can one do that without physical and/or mental action? And don't those actions represent **"works"**? I choose, therefore, not to *wade into the big weeds* of righteousness and justification. Perhaps you disagree.

39

The Resurrection

And it came to pass while they were wondering what to make of this, that behold, two men stood by them in dazzling raiment. And when the women were struck with fear and bowed their faces to the ground, they said to them: "Why do you seek the living one among the dead? He is not here but has risen." (Luke 24:2-4)

Since I followed Jesus from the Jordan to Jerusalem with my reflections, I believe it is important to now reflect on his RESURRECTION from the dead as the apex of my effort.

Interestingly, early on, the Resurrection was not generally accepted; many felt the idea of "Jesus rising from the dead" was just a product of the imagination of the apostles. As Christians, we can look to St. Paul for guidance: "For I delivered to you first of all what I also received, that Christ died for our sins according to the Scriptures, and that he was buried, and that he rose again the third day, according to the Scriptures, and that he appeared to Cephas, and after that to the eleven. Then he was seen by more than five hundred brethren at one time, many of whom are still with us, but some have fallen asleep. After that he was seen by James, then by all the apostles. And last of all, as one born out of due time, he was seen also by me. (1 Corinthians 15:3–9)

So, what is the message of the Resurrection for us? In our following Jesus, as noted previously, we read in John's Gospel where seven times Jesus stated, "I Am" in his teaching to help his disciples understand who he was and the purpose of his taking on a "human nature." Moreover, in John's Gospel, we read numerous passages where Jesus indicated **he was God**. Then, we read this in Matthew's Gospel: "From that time Jesus began to show his disciples that he must go to Jerusalem and suffer many things from the elders and Scribes and chief priests and be put to death **and on the third day rise again**." (Matthew 16:21–23)

With his Resurrection, Jesus VALIDATED who he claimed to be!

Jesus said: "Let not your hearts be troubled. You believe in God, believe also in me. In my Fathers' house there are many mansions. Were it not so, I should have told you, because I go to prepare a place for you. And if I go and prepare a place for you, **I am coming again** and I will take you to myself, that where I am there, you also may be." (John 16:2–4)

I am the **Resurrection and the LIFE!**

There is NO resurrection apart from Christ; he is life, and he confers his life on those who trust in him. Eternal Life!

Once more we look to St Paul: "But if there is no resurrection of the dead, neither has Christ risen; and if Christ has not risen, vain then is our preaching; vain too is your faith." (1 Corinthians 15:13–15)

> *But the angel spoke and said to the women, "do not be afraid; for I know that you seek Jesus who was crucified. He is not here* **for he has risen even as he said**. *Come see the place where the Lord was laid. And go quickly, tell his disciples that* **he has risen**. *And behold, he goes before you into Galilee; there you shall see him." (Matthew 28:1–7)*

Final thought: The eleven apostles went into Galilee to the mountain where Jesus had directed them to go. And when they saw him, *they worshipped him*; but some doubted. And Jesus drew near and spoke to them saying, "All power in heaven and on earth has been given to me. **Go therefore, and make disciples of all nations, baptizing them in the name of the Father, and of the Son, and the Holy Spirit, teaching them to observe all that I have commanded you**; and behold, I am with you all days even unto the consummation of the world." (Matthew 28:16–20)

WHAT DOES THE RESURRECTION MEAN TO YOU?

40

Last But Not Least

As I pointed out in previous reflections, Jesus worked 37 miracles during his time on Earth; we have studied many of them.

Biblical scholars disagree on which miracle was his *last*; most would say that it was when he healed the ear of a servant of the high priest after it was severed by a follower of Jesus during his arrest. (Luke 26:50)

I am more inclined to accept the thinking of those who would argue that his last miracle took place when he appeared to the apostles for the third time *after* his Resurrection.

Not being inclined to enter into that argument, we will, instead, study the event identified as "The Second Miraculous Catch of Fish." It is a miracle, one frequently overlooked but, I believe, offers much *food for thought*.

As usual, I feel it will be helpful to *set the scene*. We found described in Chapter 20 of John's Gospel where Jesus appeared to Mary Magdalene at the tomb the first day of the week following his Resurrection (John 20:16) AND later that same day he appeared to those gathered behind closed doors. (John 20:20–21) That brings us to our passage for today; I apologize for its length:

> *After these things, Jesus manifested himself again at the Sea of Tiberias. Now he manifested himself in this way. There were together Simon Peter and Thomas, called the Twin, and Nathanael, from Cana in Galilee, and the sons of Zebedee, and two others of his disciples. Peter said to them, "I am going fishing," They said to him, "We also are going with thee." And they went out and got into the boat.* **And that night they caught nothing.** *But when day was breaking, Jesus stood on the beach; yet the disciples did not know that it was Jesus. Then Jesus said to them, "Young men, have you any fish?" They answered him, "No." He said to them, "Cast the net to the right of the boat and you will find them." They cast therefore, and now they were unable to draw it up for the great number of fishes. The disciple whom Jesus loved said therefore to Peter,* **"It is the Lord."** *Simon Peter, therefore, hearing that it was the Lord, girt his tunic about him, for he was stripped, and threw himself into the sea. But the other disciples came with the boat (for they were not far from land, only about two hundred cubits off), dragging the net* **full of fishes.** *When, therefore, they had landed, they saw a fire ready, and a fish laid upon it, and bread. Jesus said to them, "Bring here some of the fishes that you caught just now." Simon Peter went aboard and hauled the net onto the land full of*

*LARGE fishes, one hundred and fifty-three in number. And though there were so many, the **net was not torn**. Jesus said to them, "Come and breakfast." And none of those reclining dared to ask, "Who art thou?" **knowing that it was the Lord**. And Jesus came and took the bread and gave it to them, and likewise the fish. (John 21:1–11)*

Interestingly, we began, "After these things;" but there is no clue as to a time frame. It would seem that since going to Galilee, per Jesus' instruction through Mary Magdalene, and the other women at the tomb, the apostles were uncertain as to what they should be doing; so, to go back to fishing would be the natural thing for them to do. I believe it is also worth noting that this miracle was for the *apostles only*. Perhaps, some time had passed, and Jesus felt they needed a "jolt" to get them *refocused on their task to take the Gospel to ALL Nations*. And, therefore, this miracle has a twofold meaning: To strengthen the faith of the apostles and to prepare them, especially Peter, for their *new way of life*, being **fishers of men** by following his "instructions."

And we should not overlook the fact, vividly brought out in our passage, that, as with the apostles, **without God's help we can do nothing**. And, IF we trust in the Lord our work will produce many fishes. So let us not get discouraged in our efforts to spread the "good news;" always being aware that Jesus is close by to assist us, just as he did for them that morning. And one day, God willing, we might hear, as the apostles did, "COME AND BREAKFAST."

GOOD LUCK WITH YOUR FISHING!

41

No Time to Relax

We made it through another Lenten season; Easter has come and gone. Now what?

First, let us never lose sight of the wonders of Christ's Crucifixion and Resurrection; and let us never forget that Jesus died on that cross for **our sins**. Finally, let us not take for granted the significance of that Resurrection by which he provides for us a path to heaven. We now have his promise of a new life after death, **if** we follow that path; however, let us not delude ourselves, **nothing is given**. We have been blessed with the grace of faith. As baptized Christians, we have *received the light* of Christ; and, accordingly, we are *challenged* to take that light into the world and be instruments of that light by our **actions** each and every day.

"As the body without the Spirit is dead, so Faith without works is also dead." (James 2:26)

I am reminded of what my dear mother used to tell me in my youth: "An idle mind is the Devil's workshop." So, as we begin our journey through Easter season, the question before us is: **Do we have a plan?** Winston Churchill said: "He who fails to plan is planning to fail."

In the event we struggle to sense Jesus in our daily lives, it might be helpful to recall that even those closest to him struggled after Jesus' Crucifixion and Resurrection; indeed, several did not even **recognize** him when they encountered him: Mary Magdalene met Jesus at the tomb but did not know him. (John 20:11–18) Two of his followers traveling to Emmaus met Jesus on the road but did not know him until he made his presence known *in the breaking of the bread*. (Luke: 13:35) Even when Jesus appeared to the apostles in the upper room on the first day of the week following his Resurrection, they thought he was a ghost until he showed them his hands and his side. (Luke 24:35–48)

THEY were not looking for Him; HE SOUGHT THEM OUT.

Looking ahead, as we work to formulate a *plan* that includes Jesus in our daily activities, we might be surprised to find he is already there in the people we interact with; it could be someone in our own family or that rude person in the check-out line or the driver who just took our parking space. Will we recognize him whenever or wherever we encounter Him? We are called to **keep trying**!!

As Christians, we have been given our assignment; Jesus said: "The harvest, indeed, is great, but the laborers are few. **PRAY**, therefore, the Lord of the harvest to send forth laborers into His harvest." (Matthew 9:37–38)

Aren't we challenged to be those laborers?

Perhaps you might be wondering: Where should I begin? I know there are a number of ways, but I found a good place to start was the same source used by the Fathers of the early Church:

A Layman's Thoughts on Holy Scripture

The Acts of the Apostles—Prelude—Luke

In the former book, I spoke of all that Jesus did and taught until the day on which He was taken up, after He had given commandments through the Holy Spirit to the apostles whom He had chosen. He showed also Himself alive after His passion, by many proofs, during forty days, appearing to them and speaking of the kingdom of God. And while eating with them, He charged them not to depart from Jerusalem but to wait for the promise of the Father, "of which you have heard" said He: "by My mouth; for John, indeed, baptized with water, but you shall be baptized with the Holy Spirit not many days hence…but you shall receive power when the Holy Spirit comes upon you and you shall be witnesses for me in Jerusalem, and in all Judea and Samaria and even to the very ends of the earth." And when He had said this, He was lifted up before their eyes, and a cloud took Him out of their sight.

There they **stood**! Here **we stand**! In ACTS we read where Peter sprang into action and the other ten followed: **EVANGELIZATION HAD BEGUN**!

Lord, help me to recognize you in everyone I meet today.

The final question: Will we be ready when Jesus seeks us out?

42

Pentecost

Before we undertake our study of this event, we need to lay a "verbal" foundation. We find this: He said to them, "but who do you say that I am?" Simon Peter answered and said, "Thou art the Christ, the Son of the living God." Then Jesus answered and said, "Blessed are thou, Simon Bar-Jona, for flesh and blood has not revealed this to thee but my Father in heaven. And I say to thee thou art Peter, and upon this rock **I will build my Church** and the gates of hell shall not prevail against it." (Matthew 16:16–19)

Now, you may recall we ended our reflection on the Resurrection with this: And Jesus drew near and spoke to them saying, "all power in heaven and on earth has been given to me. **Go therefore and make disciples of all nations, baptizing them in the name of the Father, and of the Son and the Holy Spirit."** (Matthew 28:18–20)

While I am sure the apostles were anxious to undertake that challenge there was a problem; they were all Jews and spoke Aramaic. Jesus knew that! So, then we read this: "And I send forth upon you the promise of my Father. But wait here in the city **until you are clothed with power from on high**." (Luke 24:48–49)

That brings us to Pentecost which is a day celebrated by Christians commemorating that event when the Holy Spirit descended on those from ALL NATIONS gathered together in Jerusalem for the Jewish Feast of Weeks.

However, the word "pentecost" has nothing to do with the Holy Spirit; it simply means "fifty" and establishes that the Feast is to be held on the fiftieth day after the Resurrection (Easter). Also, just an interesting note, the Feast of Pentecost is the ONLY Feast which is celebrated by both Jews and Christians.

Regardless, Pentecost is a fascinating story and is of utmost importance in that it signifies the *official* beginning of the spread of Christianity. It is a story worthy of our reading according to Luke:

> *And when the days of Pentecost were drawing to a close, they were **all** together in one place. And suddenly there came a sound from **heaven** as a violent wind blowing and it filled the whole house where they were sitting; and there appeared to **them** parted tongues as of fire which settled upon **each of them**. And they were **all filled with the Holy Spirit and began to speak in foreign tongues each as the Holy Spirit prompted them to speak**. Now there were staying in Jerusalem devout Jews from **every nation under heaven**. And when this sound was heard the multitude gathered and were bewildered in mind,*

*because **each** heard them speaking in his own language. (The Acts 2:1–6)*

In this way, he kept his earlier promise: "But I speak the truth to you; it is expedient for you that I depart. For, if I do not go, the Advocate will not come to you; but if I go, I will send Him to you." (John 16:7–13)

PROMISE KEPT!

Then, following his Resurrection, Jesus appeared to those gathered behind locked doors; he stood in their midst and said: "Peace be to you! As the Father has **sent** me, I also **send you**." When he had said this, he breathed upon them and said to them, "Receive the Holy Spirit; whose sins you shall forgive they are forgiven them; and whose sins you shall retain they are retained." (John 20:21–23)

From all of the above, it is clear to me that Jesus established his Church on Earth, ascended into heaven and charged his apostles with spreading his gospel message to all nations. Having done that, he prevailed upon his Father to send the Holy Spirit on OTHERS! So it is, on the Feast of Pentecost we celebrate that blessing, **not just those gathered in that room but WE, also, by our BAPTISM**. Accordingly, the instruction by Jesus to the apostles to "make disciples of all nations" falls on us, as well. Clearly, few can proclaim to the extent of preaching or teaching; so, we turn to St. Paul for guidance:

Now there are varieties of gifts but the same spirit; and there are varieties of ministries but the same Lord; and there are varieties of workings but the same God who works all things in all. Now the manifestation of the Spirit is given to everyone for profit. To one through the Spirit is given the utterance of wisdom; and to another the utterance of knowledge, according to the same Spirit; to another faith in the same Spirit; to another the gift of healing, in the one Spirit; to another the working of miracles; to another prophecy, to another distinguishing of spirits; to another various kinds of tongues; to another the interpretation of tongues. But all these things are the work of one and the same Spirit, who allots to everyone according as he will. (1 Corinthians 12:4–12)

The expectation is clear: we are ALL EXPECTED to utilize whatever talents we have received and **"produce fruit"** by the way we live our lives.

And so, let us pray: **Come Holy Spirit and kindle in us the fire of your love.**

AFTERWORD

I dare say few of us spend enough time reading and thinking about the WORDS spoken by Jesus during his, relatively, brief time on earth as found in the four gospels in the New Testament.

Personally, I am humbled and grateful that I was awakened to my need to learn more about Holy Scripture. Once I picked up my bible, I found myself being drawn to read more about Jesus' time on earth, the successes he enjoyed, the obstacles he faced and his ultimate victory over sin and death.

I found increased energy for my endeavor with the discovery of these words from Jesus: "It is the spirit that gives life, the flesh is useless. The words that I have spoken to you are spirit and life." (John 6:63)

One of the challenges I faced was deciding which of the many beautiful stories in the bible could, appropriately, be described within the parameters of my self-imposed limits on the total number reflections to be included and a reasonable length for each one.

Without regard to those constraints, I feel it is important to go beyond the gospels and end my effort with this passage:

"That I, Paul, might not become too elated, because of the abundance of the revelations, a thorn in the flesh was given to me, an angel of Satan, to beat me to keep me from being too elated. Three times I begged the Lord about this, that it might leave me, but he said to me, "My grace is sufficient for you, for the power is made perfect in weakness." (2 Corinthians 12:7–8)

It is easy to apply those WORDS to our many everyday situations:

> Success is made perfect through struggles.

> Peace is made perfect through conflict.

> Contentment is made perfect through prayer.

We should each one of us ponder what "thorn" God has placed in our life and remember his WORDS: "MY GRACE IS SUFFICIENT FOR YOU."

For those of you who might be inclined to follow in my footsteps, I want to stress how much enjoyment I got from researching the views of other scripture devotees to assist me in discerning which of my "random" thoughts met my goals of accuracy, thoroughness, and brevity. On my journey, I steadfastly sought the guidance of the Holy Spirit.

I believe I undertook this challenge for the right reasons. My sincere hope is that you enjoyed my book as much as I enjoyed writing it.

www.ingramcontent.com/pod-product-compliance
Lightning Source LLC
Chambersburg PA
CBHW061759070526
44586CB00023B/2628